DIPA MA

DIPA MA

The Life and Legacy of a Buddhist Master

Amy Schmidt

BlueBridge

Cover design by Per-Henrik Gurth

Cover photography by Janice Rubin: Dipa Ma at IMS, 1984

Parts of this book were first published as *Knee Deep in Grace*.

Library of Congress Cataloging-in-Publication Data available upon request.

ISBN: 0-9742405-5-9

The lines quoted on page 30 are from *The Dhammapada*, Chapter 16, Verse 212 (Section 4, pages 59–60), translated by The Venerable Balangoda Ananda Maitreya and revised by Rose Kramer (Omni Foundation, 1988).

Wendy Palmer's story *This Life Is in Trouble* on pages 99–100 is adapted from *The Practice of Freedom: Aikido Principles as a Spiritual Guide* by Wendy Palmer. Reprinted with permission of Rodmell Press.

Published by
B l u e B r i d g e
An imprint of
United Tribes Media Inc.
Goldens Bridge, New York

www.bluebridgebooks.com

Printed in the United States of America

10 9 8 7

Dedicated to
Dipa Ma

CONTENTS

FOREWORD

I REMEMBER DIPA MA not only as my teacher but as a woman, a mother, and a grandmother. I remember her, sitting on the floor of the house in Barre where she and her family were staying when they visited the Insight Meditation Society. She would be playing games with her young grandson Rishi, laughing, and then she would get up to instruct someone in meditation. Afterwards perhaps she might go wash her clothes by hand and hang them out to dry. She might do walking meditation, then return to the house to sit. Rishi would be running around the room, while her daughter Dipa would be cooking. And Dipa Ma would be meditating right there in the midst of all that activity. Whenever anyone sat down in front of her, she would open her eyes and shower the person with blessings. This was how Dipa Ma taught, with warmth, simplicity, and goodheartedness.

Many times I hear her voice whispering to me, challenging me to extend myself to find what I am actually capable of, especially in terms of love and compassion. She was an incredible model of kindness, the type that is born of great suffering, and a consequent, constant remembrance of what is really important. When I find myself hesitating, frightened of opening up to somebody, I see an image of her as she comes out of meditation in a chaotic room, and blesses someone. I hear her voice encouraging me. Then, filled with her blessing, I reach beyond my fears to find within me the lovingkindness she embodied so strongly.

Sharon Salzberg

INTRODUCTION

THERE MAY BE a few times in our lives when we meet a person who is so unusual that she or he transforms the way we live just by being who they are. Dipa Ma was such a person. I had first heard about her from my teacher Anagarika Munindra when I went to Bodh Gaya, India, in 1967 to practice meditation. He had trained Dipa Ma in Burma, where he had been practicing and teaching for the previous nine years. He spoke of her often as being an extraordinary yogi (meditator) with unusual attainments—many of which you will read about in this book. What he did not say in words, but which was apparent from the first time of my meeting her, was the special quality of her being that touched everyone who met her. It was a quality of the quietest peace fully suffused with love. This stillness and love were different from anything I had encountered before. They were not an ego persona, and they didn't want or need anything in return. Simply, in the absence of self, love and peace were what remained.

Dipa Ma brought forth our best efforts, not by rules but by inspiration. She showed what was possible by being what was possible—and it raised the bar of our own aspirations. She had unwavering confidence in each of our abilities to walk the path of dharma. That confidence was conveyed with a total acceptance of where we were, along with a relentless encouragement to deepen our understanding through continued practice.

Although Dipa Ma made only two trips to the West, her impact on Buddhism in America has been profound. She was the first truly accomplished woman meditation master in the Theravada tradition to teach in this country. Although she had a deep devotion to the tradition, she also had a fierce understanding that the spiritual accomplishments of women (and householders, at that) could be in every way equal to—and often deeper than—those of the predominantly male religious hierarchy. In this way, too, Dipa Ma became a powerful role model here for women and men alike. The effect she had on so many practitioners is still rippling throughout the dharma community.

I am delighted and grateful that Amy Schmidt has brought forth this wonderful book. It is a chance for many of us to recall stories and encounters with Dipa Ma and an opportunity for others to meet Dipa Ma for the first time.

Joseph Goldstein

PREFACE:
DISCOVERING DIPA MA

LONG BEFORE I ever heard her name, Dipa Ma was calling to me.

When I was nineteen, someone handed me a copy of Herman Hesse's *Siddhartha*. I read it four times and underlined almost every sentence. The book offered me hope. It said—and I desperately wanted it to be true—that there was a way out of suffering, that it was possible to be free in this human life. I began to practice Transcendental Meditation, but I didn't find my way to the dharma, or Buddhist teaching, until five years later. At a back-alley coffeehouse in Seattle called the Allegro, I saw a flyer advertising a dharma group posted on their bulletin board. I was curious, so I dropped in. Someone instructed me in sitting meditation.

Immediately I sensed that I'd found something deep and meaningful in this practice, something I knew I had to stay with. A teacher from Thailand visited the group and spoke about enlightenment. He said it was the goal of meditation, and that it was "indescribable," beyond body and mind, beyond all suffering. What intrigued me more than what he said, however, was what remained unspoken: the mystical silence surrounding his words, the deep calm in his eyes. That night, walking home in the rain, I was brought to a halt by a strong sensation. With the rain pouring down my face in the darkness, I vowed to dedicate the rest of my life to finding enlightenment. No matter how long it took—no matter what it took—I knew

I would not stop until I had experienced that peace for myself.

From time to time, Buddhist teachers came to visit our group: a man who had been ordained in Burma (now Myanmar), several monks from the Thai tradition. Invariably these were male teachers who talked about their male teachers. "Where are the women in this tradition?" I wondered, "Where are *my* mentors?"

Hoping to learn more about women in Buddhism, I began to read the Buddhist texts, which left me more discouraged. Not only were women seldom mentioned, but in general the ancient writings presented a disparaging view of us. Like other women of that era, I abandoned my notions of female Buddhist role models and just dove into my own practice.

After five years of strenuous effort, I began to feel the need for longer periods of intensive practice. Several friends told me about the three-month retreat held every fall at the Insight Meditation Society (IMS) in Barre, Massachusetts. I applied and was accepted. Three months of silence—many of my friends thought I was crazy. The year was 1989.

The retreat center, founded by meditation teachers Sharon Salzberg, Joseph Goldstein, Jack Kornfield, and others, is surrounded by woods and fields. The main building is a stately old brick structure, a lieutenant governor's private mansion built in 1911. After the bustle of unpacking boxes and meeting my Swiss roommate, I took a guided tour of the maze of buildings where I would be living and practicing for the next ninety days. As I looked around the place, I noticed figures of the Buddha and pictures of teachers, inspiring icons of spiritual encouragement placed thoughtfully in every nook and cranny. All were images of men.

Then, suddenly, off in the corner of room M101, I spotted a photograph of an Indian woman dressed in white, seated like a puff of white cloud on a green summer lawn. She wore heavy-rimmed eyeglasses repaired with a strip of white tape. Behind the glasses was the most serene, loving gaze I had ever seen. There was no name on the picture, but I knew that I was looking at a great master, a woman who had found deep freedom. I wondered if the teachers would tell us about her. I wondered if she might be my mentor.

I didn't have to wait long for an answer. A few days into the retreat, the teachers began to speak about the woman in the picture. Born Nani Bala Barua, but known to all as Dipa Ma ("mother of Dipa"), she had died only two weeks before. Each of the five teachers had known her personally and had loved her deeply. Two of them had been her students for nearly twenty years. Grief was still fresh in their hearts. I felt dismayed that I would never get to meet this woman. Then it dawned on me: through the stories I was hearing and the inspiration they imparted, Dipa Ma was already becoming my mentor.

I felt a strong kinship with her: there were so many similarities between her story and my own. She had experienced profound suffering in her life when, at the age of twelve, she was separated from her family and married off according to Indian custom. My own world also changed abruptly and irrevocably at the age of twelve: I woke up one morning to discover that my mother, to whom I was deeply attached, had tried to commit suicide the night before. Even though she did not succeed until several years later, the effect on me was utterly devastating. As it had happened for Dipa Ma, my childhood ended suddenly, literally overnight. Other events in my teens and twenties seemed to parallel some of the losses and struggles Dipa Ma experienced before she discovered meditation practice.

As a child I had loved the stories my mother told me about African Americans who, despite the odds, rose above their suffering to become great leaders and teachers. Mahalia Jackson, Dr. Martin Luther King Jr., Malcolm X, Paul Robeson, Marian Anderson, Frederick Douglass, Rosa Parks: these were my childhood heroes and heroines. How, I wanted to know, had Dipa Ma, an ordinary housewife, overcome not only personal difficulties but also the patriarchal constraints of Asian culture, and then gone on to practice and teach in ways highly uncommon for her time? Although she never identified herself as a feminist or a minority leader, Dipa Ma reminded me of my childhood heroes in her example of strength in the face of adversity.

I was eager to follow in her footsteps. I wanted to know *everything* about her. I met with Joseph Goldstein at the end of the three-month retreat and asked if he or any other teacher was planning to write about Dipa Ma. No, he said, no one that he knew of. He certainly didn't have the time to do it. Then, with characteristic ebullience, he said, "You should do it!"

For days I pondered his suggestion. How could I possibly write about someone I had never met? Several friends pointed out that of the millions who followed the Buddha's teachings in the twenty-five hundred years since he lived, only a handful knew him personally. The same, of course, is true for Jesus, Muhammad, and other spiritual leaders. Their stories are their living texts.

So I began my search for Dipa Ma through the accounts of those who had known her. For eight years, I collected stories about her from her students throughout the United States and in India and Myanmar. Every step of the journey, every meeting and every parting, every conversation and remembrance, was linked by love: love of Dipa Ma, love of the Buddhist path, love of this precious life.

The Buddha described the spiritual teachings as "beautiful in the beginning, beautiful in the middle, and beautiful in the end." As I listened to people's stories, Dipa Ma's teaching manifested that beauty again and again. Even in death, she lives on in people's hearts. Many students say they feel that she continues to guide their practice. Some who have never met her report that she helps them in their meditation or visits them in dreams. Some say they hear her voice, others that they feel her presence. For many years now, I have heard accounts of how Dipa Ma continues to guide people. Through these accounts and my own experiences, I feel certain that the power of her practice is still available to each one of us. No matter how lost we feel within ourselves, or how desperate the world situation seems, if we call upon her, she usually appears from the inside, showing us the truth which is always here.

May these stories guide you on your spiritual journey. May all beings be free.

PART ONE

DIPA MA'S EXTRAORDINARY LIFE

CHAPTER I

BORN INTO BUDDHISM

"There is nothing to cling to in this world."

NANI BALA BARUA was born on March 25, 1911, in an East Bengal village near the Burmese border. The Chittagong region was notable for its mix of religious traditions, with Hindus, Muslims, and Buddhists living harmoniously side by side. The indigenous Buddhist culture there is perhaps the only extant community dating back to the Buddha in an unbroken line.

Nani's family belonged to the Bengali Barua clan, descendants of the original Buddhists of India. Although the practice of meditation had mostly faded away by the time Nani was born, some families still observed Buddhist rituals and customs. Among them were her father, Purnachandra Barua, and her mother, Prasanna Kumari.

The eldest of six children, Nani was close to her siblings and the favorite child in her extended family. Nani and her mother, both very short and fair-skinned, enjoyed an especially close relationship. Nani remembered her mother as quiet and affectionate, her father a man of firm principle who never yielded to anything that he didn't think was right. In spite of his stern manner, Nani's relationship with him was also one of fondness.

The tradition of dana (generosity) was commonly practiced in Nani's home, with her parents giving to Buddhist monks, Hindu Brahmins, and anyone who asked for alms. It was from her parents that the young girl learned the meaning of giving to others—that when you give, there is no distinction. You give to everybody.

As a child, Nani showed an exceptional interest in Buddhist ritual. She enjoyed going to temples and serving the monks. Although children were usually kept away from the monks on their begging rounds, because of her strong fascination, Nani was allowed to offer them food and alms, wash their feet, and sit with them while they ate.

Nani kept to herself and did not seek the company of other children. She often played with dolls, but she was particularly fond of making Buddha statues. While most little Indian girls were pretend-cooking, her fantasy world involved creating food offerings and collecting flowers for the Buddha, preparing the altar, and performing religious ceremonies. The Barua household was near a lake with a brightly colored pagoda at one end, and Nani often went there to make her offerings. She recalled that her devotion came naturally, that her parents by no means urged it upon her.

Not only did Nani show no interest in cooking, but she showed little interest in eating. Rarely could her perplexed mother coax Nani to sit down to a regular meal. Instead, Nani would eat a piece of fruit or a biscuit. She often asked her parents, "Do you feel hungry? What is hunger?"

Her appetite for knowledge, on the other hand, was insatiable. Although it was not customary for girls in her village to go to school, Nani could not be kept away. Even when she was ill and told to stay home for the day, she would steal off to the classroom. Evenings often found her sitting around the table with her father, engaging him in discussion about her school texts, although most children rarely brought their studies home.

In the India of the time, a girl's childhood ended early. Those who did attend school were not allowed to continue after the fifth grade. In accordance with the norms of her culture, Nani was to be married before the onset of menstruation. Thus, at the age of twelve, she was taken from school and married to a man of twenty-five. Her fiancé, Rajani Ranjan Barua, was an engineer from the neighboring village of Silghata. As was the custom, after the marriage ceremony Nani was immediately sent to live with her new in-laws. She missed her parents terribly. To make matters worse, one week after they were married, her husband left to resume his job in Burma. Nani was left alone with her demanding in-laws, of whom she was quite afraid. She was allowed occasional visits to her parents, but then her in-laws would take her away again.

After two unhappy years, at age fourteen, Nani was put on a boat to Rangoon (now Yangon) to begin a life in a new country with a man whom she had known for no more than a week. Stepping off the boat, the timid country girl was shocked by her new surroundings. Rangoon was a noisy, strange place with a sea of unfamiliar faces and a language she could not understand. Nani was extremely lonely at first, frequently crying for her homeland and her family.

Married life, too, presented challenges. Although she had been carefully instructed by her mother and aunts about how to run a household, no one had ever said a word about sex.

Her husband was the first to tell her, and the girl's reaction was to feel shocked, nervous, and terribly ashamed. For the first year of married life, she was terrified of her husband. During that year, Rajani remained unfailingly gentle and supportive of his wife, never forcing himself on her. Eventually, as trust developed between them, Nani came to see him as a rare human being. Over the next few years, the two of them fell deeply in love. In later years, Nani often said that she considered Rajani her first teacher.

Their happy relationship, however, was marred by one extremely painful problem. The traditional expectation for a young Indian wife is that she bear a child, preferably a son, within the first year of marriage. But year after year passed without Nani conceiving. She tried going to doctors and healers, but no one could find the reason for her inability to conceive. This became a source of great shame and sorrow to her. Fortunately, Rajani remained caring, loving, and patient, without ever pushing Nani or criticizing her for failing to bear a child.

Although Rajani accepted the absence of offspring, his family and neighbors in India did not. Concerned that Nani was ruining their lineage, they lured Rajani back to Chittagong under the pretext of an illness in the family. Once home, Rajani was informed that a new wife was waiting for him and that arrangements had been made for him to marry immediately. Rajani refused. "When I married Nani," he informed his relatives, "I did not tell her that she must have children or I would leave her. This was not a condition of our marriage. Therefore it is not fair that I should leave her now."

Rajani returned to Burma and told Nani never to worry again about having children. He suggested that she treat every person she met as her own child—advice that would manifest in remarkable ways many years later.

At the age of eighteen, Nani learned that her mother had died suddenly. Despite having had a premonitory dream of her mother's death, she was terribly shocked by the news. She'd seen her mother only twice since moving to Burma. The heartache of that loss was to remain with her for many years. Then, immediately following her mother's death, Nani was stricken with typhoid fever. The disease was misdiagnosed and mistreated, and Nani was hospitalized for many months.

Nani's mother left behind an eighteen-month-old boy named Bijoy. Her father, unable to care for the baby, offered Nani and Rajani the chance to bring up this youngest brother as their own child, and Bijoy was sent to live with them in Rangoon.

Nani and Rajani were actively involved in the Buddhist community. In addition to following the five Buddhist precepts—to refrain from killing and causing harm; from taking what isn't freely offered; from sexual misconduct; from false speech; and from using intoxicants—they maintained daily rituals (chanting the sutras [teachings]), sponsored two community feasts a year, and offered alms to the local monks. They were especially known for their generosity: they paid for the schooling of children from needy families and offered their own home as shelter for the homeless.

From the day she arrived in Rangoon, Nani felt a strong desire to meditate. Even though girls typically did not study meditation, she repeatedly asked Rajani for permission to learn it. Each time she asked, he would suggest that she wait until she was older, following the traditional Indian custom of postponing spiritual practice until later years when the householder's duties are fulfilled.

Although she spoke no Burmese, Nani found ways to pursue a Buddhist education in her adopted country. Whenever

she could find a Bengali religious book, she would read and study it on her own. For other books, she enlisted the help of her thirteen-year-old nephew, Sunil, who would translate the classical Buddhist texts from Burmese to Bengali. Sunil was astonished by Nani's studiousness and how well she remembered everything that he read to her. (Years later, when she had completed a battery of psychological tests, her intelligence was found to be highly exceptional.)

In 1941, when Nani was thirty, Burma was attacked and occupied by Japanese troops. It was a time of fear, scarcity, and hardship. At the war's end in 1945, Bijoy, now grown, returned to India to start his own family. With an empty house and both parents dead, Nani thought, "Now must be the time to learn meditation."

Then a miracle occurred: after more than twenty years of trying to conceive a child, Nani discovered that she was pregnant. She was thirty-five years old when she joyfully gave birth to a baby girl. After three months, however, the child sickened and died. Overwhelmed with grief, Nani developed heart disease.

Four years later, she was blessed with another pregnancy. Again it was a girl, whom she named Dipa. It was at this time that Nani was given her nickname, "Dipa Ma," or "Mother of Dipa." Since Dipa means "light," Nani's new name also meant "Mother of Light."

Dipa was a healthy toddler when her mother became pregnant yet again, this time with the all-important boy child. This infant died at birth, once more plunging Dipa Ma into inconsolable grief. In desperation, she demanded the right to learn meditation to relieve her sorrow. Again, her husband said that she was too young. She threatened to sneak out of the house, and Rajani and several neighbors began to keep watch over her.

Their vigil soon became unnecessary. Stricken with hyper-
tension, Dipa Ma wasn't able to leave her bed, much less the
house, for several years. During that period, she fully expected
to die at any moment. Single-handedly, Rajani nursed his wife
and took charge of toddler Dipa, while continuing to work full-
time as an engineer. The stress of the situation eventually overwhelmed him. One night in 1957, he came home from work
and told his wife that he was feeling ill. Within hours, he was
dead of a heart attack.

CHAPTER 2

AWAKENING

"What can I take with me when I die?"

WITHIN TEN YEARS, Dipa Ma had lost two children, her husband, and her health. In her mid-forties, she was a widow with a seven-year-old daughter to raise on her own. Both of her parents were dead, India was far away, and she was overwhelmed with grief and confusion.

"I didn't know what to do, where to go, or how to live," she said. "I had nothing and no one to call my own." Months went by, and all she could do was cry, holding a photo of Rajani in her lap. During the next few years, her health continued to decline. Her condition became so serious that she felt her only hope of survival would be to practice meditation. She reflected on the irony of her situation. When she was young, healthy, and eager to meditate, she had been prevented from doing so. Now, responsible for a child and totally exhausted, in despair and facing death, she felt that she had no other option, that she would die of a broken heart unless she did something about the state of her mind.

She asked herself, "What can I take with me when I die?" She looked around at her dowry, her silk saris and gold jewelry, even at her daughter. "As much as I loved her, I knew I couldn't take her. . . . So I said, 'Let me go to the meditation center. Maybe I can find something there I can take with me when I die.'"

At this lowest point in her life, the Buddha appeared to her in a dream. A luminous presence, he softly chanted a verse from the Dhammapada, originally offered as consolation to a father grieving the death of his son:

> *Clinging to what is dear brings sorrow,*
> *Clinging to what is dear brings fear.*
> *To one who is entirely free from endearment,*
> *There is no sorrow or fear.*

When Dipa Ma awoke, she felt clear and calm. She knew she must learn to meditate no matter what the state of her health. She understood the Buddha's advice: if she wanted true peace, she had to practice until she was free from all attachment and sorrow.

Although she had performed Buddhist rituals all her life, Dipa Ma knew little about what meditation practice actually entailed. Intuitively, however, she was drawn to the ancient path that promised freedom from suffering. Unlike concentration practices in which attention is fixed on a single object, vipassana (insight) meditation focuses on the constantly changing nature of experience. "Insight" refers to clearly seeing into the three characteristics of experience: its impermanence, its unsatisfactoriness, and the absence of an inherent self. The Buddha taught that through meditation, it is possible to break through the illusions that limit our lives. Liberation, or enlightenment, according to Buddhist teaching, lies in experiencing the true nature of existence.

Dipa Ma made arrangements to go to the Kamayut Meditation Center in Rangoon. Everything her husband had left her—her property, her jewelry, all of her material goods—she gave to her next-door neighbor, saying, "Please take whatever I have, and use it to care for Dipa." She expected never to return. If she was going to die anyway, she reasoned, it might as well be at the meditation center.

Dipa Ma's first retreat did not go as she expected. Once at the center, she was given a room and basic instruction. She began to practice in the early morning hours, first focusing her attention on the breath, then noting the sensations, thoughts, and emotions arising in her body and mind as she sat. As the day wore on, her concentration deepened. That afternoon, she started to walk to the meditation hall to meet with her teacher. Suddenly she stopped, unable to move. She wasn't sure why, she only knew that she couldn't go forward or pick up her foot. She stood there, puzzled but not particularly distressed, for several minutes. Finally, she looked down and saw that a large dog had clamped its teeth around her leg. Her concentration had become so deep, even in the first hours of practice, that she had not felt it.

Jolted from her concentrated state, Dipa Ma called for help and tried to shake her leg free. The dog would not let go, but finally some monks managed to pull it away. Even though they assured her that the animal was not rabid, Dipa Ma was afraid of dying—ironically, since she'd come to the meditation center to die—and she made her way to a hospital where she was given the first of a series of daily rabies injections. Going back and forth to the hospital meant that she missed eating; in South Asian monastic tradition, a single meal is served each day, and it must be eaten before noon. Soon Dipa Ma had become so weak that the monks suggested that she return home to recuperate.

At home, her young daughter, upset by her mother's abrupt departure, would not let her out of her sight. Dipa Ma felt that her one opportunity for enlightenment had passed. Frequently she wept out of sheer frustration.

She didn't give up her meditation practice, however. Using the beginning instructions she'd been given on her short retreat, she meditated patiently at home for several years, making time whenever she could. She had faith that eventually she would find another chance to go on retreat.

That opportunity came when Dipa Ma learned that a family friend and Buddhist teacher, Anagarika Munindra, was living at a nearby meditation center. ("Anagarika" means "non-householder," or one who has left home to follow the spiritual path). She invited him to her home and related her meditation experience to him over tea. Munindra encouraged her to come to Thathana Yeiktha, the meditation center where he himself was deepening his practice under the tutelage of the Venerable Mahasi Sayadaw, the most renowned monk, scholar, and meditation master in Burma at that time. Thus Dipa Ma was offered a rare opportunity: to learn from a great teacher, guided by a family friend in her native language. Around the same time, her sister Hema and her family came to Burma so now her daughter, Dipa, would be able to live with her aunt, uncle, and cousins while Dipa Ma was at the meditation center.

Dipa Ma embarked on her second retreat in a very different frame of mind—less urgent and impulsive, more planned and thoughtful. Although she had been an insomniac since the death of Rajani, now she found that she could not stay awake. By the third day, however, she was able to attain a deep state of concentration and the need for sleep vanished, along with the desire to eat. Munindra, concerned that her concentration was out of balance, requested that she attend Mahasi Sayadaw's weekly talk, even though she couldn't understand Burmese. She didn't want to go, but Munindra insisted, and to please him, she went.

On the way to the talk, Dipa Ma began to experience heart palpitations. Feeling very weak, she ended up on her hands and knees, crawling up the stairs to the hall. She didn't understand the talk but continued her meditation practice. After the talk Dipa Ma found that she couldn't stand up. She felt stuck in her seated posture, her body stiff, immobilized by the depth of her concentration.

In the following days, Dipa Ma's practice deepened dramatically as she moved rapidly through the classical stages of the "progress of insight" that are said to precede enlightenment, according to the teachings of the Theravada Buddhist (South Asian) tradition. She experienced a brilliant light, followed by the feeling that everything around her was dissolving. Her body, the floor, everything was in pieces, broken and empty. That gave way to intense mental and physical pain, with an excruciating burning and constricting in her body. She felt that she would burst with pressure.

Then something extraordinary happened. A simple moment—it was daytime, she was sitting on the floor, practicing among a group of meditators—an instantaneous transition took place, so quiet and delicate, that it seemed as if nothing at all had happened. Of this luminous instant Dipa Ma was later to say simply, "I did not know," and yet in it her life had been profoundly and irrevocably transformed.

After over three decades of searching for freedom, at the age of fifty-three, after six days of practice, Dipa Ma reached the first stage of enlightenment. (The Theravada tradition recognizes four phases of enlightenment, each producing distinct, recognizable changes in the mind.) Almost immediately her blood pressure returned to normal and her heart palpitations diminished. Previously unable to climb the meditation center stairs, this ascent was now effortless, and she could walk at any pace. As the Buddha had predicted in her dream, the grief she had borne day and night vanished. Her constant fearfulness was gone, leaving her with an unprecedented equanimity and a clear understanding that she could handle anything.

Dipa Ma continued to practice at Thathana Yeiktha for two more months, then returned to her home in Rangoon. After a few weeks, she embarked on a year of frequent trips back and forth to the center. At her next retreat, she experienced another breakthrough after only five days of meditation. The path leading to this insight was similar to the first, except that it was marked by even more pain and suffering. After reaching the second stage of enlightenment, her physical and mental condition were transformed yet again; her restlessness decreased, while her physical stamina increased.

Those who knew Dipa Ma were fascinated by her transformation. Almost overnight she had changed from a sickly, dependent, grief-stricken woman into a healthy, independent, radiant being. Dipa Ma told those around her: "You have seen me. I was disheartened and broken down due to the loss of my husband and children and due to disease. I suffered so much. I could not walk properly. But now how are you finding me? All my disease is gone. I am refreshed, and there is nothing in my mind. There is no sorrow, no grief. I am quite happy. If you come to meditate, you will also be happy. There is no magic. Only follow the instructions."

Inspired by Dipa Ma's example, her friends and family came to practice at the center. The first to arrive were her sister, Hema, and a close friend, Khuki Ma. Although Hema was the mother of eight children, five of whom still lived at home, she made time to practice with her sister for almost a year. Later, Dipa Ma's daughter, Dipa, and several of Hema's daughters joined them. They were a sight to behold: two middle-aged mothers and their teenage daughters meditating among the austere, saffron-clad monks. Meditation centers did not normally accommodate female retreatants, and their living quarters were rustic, hovel-like rooms in a remote corner of the property. Hema's daughter, Daw Than Myint, recalled that they had to climb through the bushes and scramble up a hill to get to their interviews with Munindra.

During school holidays, Dipa Ma and Hema might have as many as six children between them. Despite the close family atmosphere, the rules were strict. "We would eat in silence together as a family," remembered Daw Than Myint, "and we would not look up at each other. It was very different!" During this phenomenal year of practice, all six children of the Barua clan, four girls and two boys, achieved at least the first stage of enlightenment. The young Dipa's commitment to meditation practice was especially gratifying to her mother, who wanted to give her daughter something of enduring value, the "priceless gift." Again and again she would tell Dipa that meditation offered the only way to peace.

Dipa Ma's sister, Hema, was also adept in meditation practice and had progressed rapidly to the same level as Dipa Ma.

Daw Than Myint recalled the powerful effect meditation had on her mother:

> When I arrived home from college vacation, my mother was not there to greet me. This was very unusual, because she never stayed away from home long. My brothers and sisters informed me that she was at the meditation center. When I went to the center, I saw her sitting next to Munindra, very cool and calm and not acknowledging me. I was impressed. I wanted to be aloof like that. I decided if meditation can change my mother, it must be very powerful, and so I must do this also. Of course I later found that meditation was not about being cool and aloof.

Unfortunately, not everyone in the family was so enthusiastic about Hema's changes:

> My father was upset that she was not doing housework; she was just sitting, sitting, sitting, so he threatened to tell the Venerable Mahasi Sayadaw. My mother said, "Fine." When he went to talk to the Sayadaw, the Sayadaw convinced him to begin his own meditation. Soon he gained some insight, and he never bothered my mother again about sitting too much.

In 1965, Dipa Ma was drawn into a new dimension of spiritual practice. In anticipation of Munindra's return to India, the Venerable Mahasi Sayadaw told his student that since he was going back to "the land of siddhis" (psychic powers), he should know something about them. He wanted to train Munindra in the siddhis, but Munindra was too involved in

teaching to undertake siddhi practice himself. Instead, Munindra decided to train others, partly as an experiment to prove that the siddhis were real. For this purpose he chose his most advanced students, Dipa Ma and her family, and trained them directly from the *Visuddhimagga*. Munindra knew that psychic powers are not only amoral, but also potentially seductive. There is a great risk of their misuse unless a student's moral development is secure. Dipa Ma was chosen not only for her powers of concentration but also for her impeccable morality.

Dipa Ma, Hema, and three of their daughters were introduced to the practices of dematerialization, body-doubling, cooking food without fire, mind-reading, visitation of the heaven and hell realms, time travel, knowledge of past lives, and more. Dipa Ma was the most adept of all Munindra's students, and the most playful. It has been said that she nonchalantly arrived at her interviews with Munindra by walking through a wall or spontaneously materializing out of thin air, and that she came to master all five categories of supernatural abilities (see chapter 9).

In 1966, after Munindra's departure for India, Dipa Ma became sought after as a guide in meditation and began teaching in Rangoon. She deeply enjoyed offering to others the peace that she had found for herself, and she persuaded many friends and relatives to join her in practice.

Dipa Ma's first formal student was her neighbor Malati Barua, a widow trying to raise six young children alone. Malati presented an interesting challenge: she was eager to meditate but unable to leave her house. Dipa Ma, believing that enlightenment was possible in any environment, devised practices that her new student could carry out at home. In one such practice, she taught Malati to steadfastly notice the sucking sensation of the infant at her breast, with complete presence of mind, for the duration of each nursing period. This amounted to hours each day and, as Dipa Ma had hoped, Malati attained the first stage of enlightenment without ever leaving her home.

Thus Dipa Ma began her career of leading householders to wisdom in the midst of their busy lives.

UNSHAKEABLE PEACE

"I am perfectly at peace now. Whatever comes I will embrace."

IN 1967, THE Burmese government ordered all foreigners, including Indian émigrés, to leave the country. Dipa Ma was in a quandary about whether to stay or go. The monks assured her that she could get special permission to remain in Rangoon as a teacher, and that her daughter could also remain in the country. That was an unprecedented honor for a foreigner, much less a woman and single mother.

She reflected on the possibility of staying, but the political situation, especially in Rangoon, grew worse. Her concern for the quality of Dipa's education finally convinced her that it was time to leave. In India, she decided, Dipa could reconnect with her roots and also pursue higher education in her native Bengali. They moved to a relative's house in the suburbs of Calcutta (now Kolkata). In her new surroundings, Dipa Ma missed the company of like-minded people. She invited neighborhood women to practice meditation, but they were not interested.

After a year, mother and daughter moved to a tiny apartment in an old building above a metal-grinding shop in the center of the old quarter of Calcutta. It had a closet-sized kitchen (three feet by six feet) with one charcoal burner on the floor, no running water (water had to be carried up four flights of stairs), and a communal toilet for several families. Dipa Ma slept on a thin straw mat. Although Dipa was attending university on government grants, they had no income and got by on the goodwill offerings of family members.

Eventually, word spread through the Bengali community that an accomplished meditation teacher, one who could "bring results," had arrived from Burma. Although many families observed Buddhist rituals, meditation was still foreign to the average layperson. Dipa Ma offered something new and different: an actual spiritual practice. One by one, Calcutta housewives began to arrive at her doorstep.

Presenting tough but effective lessons for people who wanted to meditate in the midst of busy lives as householders, Dipa Ma taught her students to use every moment as an opportunity for practice. Mindfulness, she said, could be applied to every activity: speaking, ironing, cooking, shopping, caring for children. "The whole path of mindfulness," she repeated tirelessly, "is this: 'Whatever you are doing, be aware of it.'" Dipa Ma had so much faith in the power of practice amid the hubbub of home life that one admirer dubbed her "The Patron Saint of Householders." When asked about the difference between formal meditation practice and daily life, she adamantly insisted, "You cannot separate meditation from life."

Everything she asked of her students Dipa Ma did herself, and more: adhering to the five precepts, sleeping only four hours a night, meditating many hours every day. Students were expected to report to her on their practice twice a week and to undertake periods of self-guided retreat during the year. While most Calcuttans love discussion and talk, Dipa Ma was often silent, or spoke only a few simple phrases when she taught. Her students were able to take refuge in the silence and the unshakeable peace that she provided. "She was one of the few people in my life in whose presence I have gone quiet," one student recalled. "I was able to rest in her silence, like resting under a large shade tree."

The family's one-room apartment had to serve as a bedroom and living space for Dipa Ma, her daughter, and later also for her daughter's son, Rishi. It was also a teaching space for the students, both Indians and Westerners, who began arriving. Sometimes Dipa Ma's room would be so crammed with students that they had to stand outside in the hallway and on the balcony. With a continual stream of visitors from early morning until late at night, Dipa Ma never refused anyone, no matter how tired she was. When her daughter urged her to take more time for herself, she insisted, "They are hungry for the dharma, so let them come."

Even ordained monks sought her guidance as a teacher. The Venerable Rastrapala Mahathera, who by then had been a monk for eighteen years, recalled that some disapproved of his choice of teachers, asking why, after completing a doctoral degree, he would practice meditation under a woman. "I don't know the way," he explained, "but she knows, so I will take help from her. I don't regard her as a woman. I think of her only as my teacher." He did a retreat under her guidance and experienced for himself what he'd only read about for eighteen years. Dipa Ma gave him her blessing to teach, and six months later, in 1970, he established the first insight meditation center in India, the well-known International Meditation Center in Bodh Gaya.

Dipa Ma's daughter witnessed many transformations in the community of students. When students first started meditating, their behavior was full of restlessness, anger, gossip, and harsh speech. After some months of practice, such behaviors subsided. Male students who had killed fish and animals gradually gave up hunting because of Dipa Ma's influence.

Jack Engler, who went to India in the mid-1970s to further his own meditation practice and to complete his doctoral research on Buddhist meditation, noted that even people living in proximity to Dipa Ma were affected by her presence:

> *When she first moved into her apartment complex, it was a pretty noisy and contentious place, with a lot of bickering, arguing, and yelling among the tenants, amplified by the open courtyard. Everyone knew everyone else's business because it was being shouted back and forth all the time. Within six months of her moving in, the whole place had quieted down and people were starting to get along with each other for the first time. Her presence, and the way she dealt with people – quietly, calmly, gently, treating them with kindness and respect, setting limits and challenging their behavior when necessary but out of concern for everyone's welfare, not out of anger or simple desire for her personal comfort— set an example and made it impossible to carry on in the angry, contentious way they had before. It was the simple force of her presence: you couldn't act like that around her. You just didn't.*

Joseph Goldstein was the first American student to be introduced to Dipa Ma. In 1967, he had met Munindra while staying at the Burmese meditation center in Bodh Gaya. Munindra later told Joseph that he had someone special for him to meet and brought him to Dipa Ma. Their bond developed into a loving mother-son relationship until her death twenty years later. Joseph recalled one of his first visits to her apartment:

> *To get to her small rooms on the top floor, you had to go down a narrow dark hallway and then up many dark flights of stairs. But when you got to her rooms, they felt filled with light. The feeling was wonderful. And when I would leave, it was as if I was floating down the streets of Calcutta, floating through the dirt and crowds. It was a very magical and sacred experience.*

In the early 1970s, Joseph introduced his friend Sharon Salzberg to Dipa Ma. A similar long-lasting bond was formed. Dipa Ma adopted both Sharon and Joseph like her own children. Sharon recalls how Dipa Ma kept photo albums of all of them together. They would drink tea, look at the albums, and talk about dharma. Sharon and Joseph both remember Dipa Ma as "the most loving person I have ever met."

Jack Kornfield, who met Dipa Ma in the late 1970s, recalls his first encounter with her:

> *I had been a monk for a while, and I was used to bowing to teachers, so I started to bow to her. I felt a little bit awkward—she wasn't a monk, she was a householder— but she just picked me up off the floor and gave me this great big bear hug, which is how she greeted me every time I saw her. It was wonderful. It was as if she was saying, "None of this bowing stuff, I'm not the big teacher that we have to make a big deal about." Just a huge hug.*

Jack, Joseph, and Sharon, now all teaching in America, told their own students about Dipa Ma. Their students told others, who in turn told still others. Dipa Ma was a curious entity to Westerners: physically she was almost invisible, a frail little elderly woman poking out of her white sari like "a little bug wrapped up in cotton," as one put it. Yet spiritually she was a giant. Entering her presence felt like walking into a force field where magical things could happen: perceptual changes, mind-to-mind communication, and spontaneous states of deep concentration.

In 1980 (and again in 1984), Joseph, Sharon, and Jack Kornfield invited Dipa Ma to teach during the annual three-month retreat at Insight Meditation Society. Even though Dipa Ma was sixty-nine, in poor health, and uncomfortable with airplane travel, she agreed to make the long journey to America, bringing along her daughter, her toddler grandson, and a translator.

The cultural gap for Dipa Ma was enormous. She was completely unfamiliar with ordinary details of American daily life, for example, that water for bathing is dispensed from a shower, that dogs live inside and are fed from bowls, that Corn Flakes and milk are eaten with a spoon, that boxes on the street spit out money when you press buttons. Sharon Salzberg related this anecdote:

> *Dipa Ma lived simply and didn't understand Western technology. The first time we brought her to the States, we were showing her grocery stores and this and that. We took her to what was then one of the first ATM machines, where you put in your card, punch in your code, and the money comes out. She's standing there*

*outside the wall of the bank, and we do our whole thing,
and she's just standing there shaking her head saying,
"Oh, it's so sad, it's so sad." We said, "What's so sad?"
And she said, "That poor person who has to sit inside
that wall all day, no light and no air, and you stick in
the card and they read it and they hand you your money."*

*So we said, "No, no, there is nobody in there, there
is just this process that happens." And she said, "Ah,
that's like anatta [the absence of self]." And we said,
"Right." Then she began to elucidate, right in that
moment, the teaching of anatta. Not only the absence
of a core being somehow in control of this process,
demanding that the body and the mind act according
to its whim or will or wish, but also that great sense of
interconnectedness, of transparency, of oneness that
comes when we look deeply, deeply inside of ourselves.*

Although Dipa Ma's teaching experience had not included
sitting on a platform tethered to a microphone in front of a
large hall of students, she attempted to accommodate her
American hosts. Unused to the cold weather of New England,
she would arrive in the meditation hall, as one student remembers, "so wrapped up in coats and shawls that you didn't know
who it was or what it was." She was fond of addressing her
audience with the refrain, "You are all my dharma children. I
could not neglect your call to come here."

While health problems prevented her return to the United
States after the 1984 trip, Dipa Ma continued to teach from
her Calcutta apartment until her death five years later. She died
on the evening of September 1, 1989, at the age of seventy-eight. Her death came unexpectedly. When Dipa returned from

work that evening, her mother wasn't feeling well. Dipa asked
if she should call a doctor. Dipa Ma hesitantly agreed, and their
neighbor Sandip Mutsuddi went to find the doctor but couldn't
locate him. When Sandip returned, he sat down next to Dipa
Ma and began to massage her arm. He recalled:

> *Then Ma asked me to touch her head, so I touched her*
> *head and I started chanting the sutras she taught me.*
> *When she heard me chanting, she bowed with her hands*
> *in prayer. She bowed toward the Buddha and did not*
> *get up. So we both lifted her off the floor and found that*
> *her breathing had stopped. She had died in her bow to*
> *the Buddha. Her face was very calm and at peace.*

Nearly four hundred people attended Dipa Ma's funeral
several days later. Her body lay on an open cot. One by one,
students filed past, laying garlands on their teacher's body until
she was completely covered with flowers.

DIPA MA'S SPIRITUAL PATH

TO THE EDGE AND BEYOND

"You can do anything you want to do."

As IN THE example of Dipa Ma's life, the spiritual path is a journey of transformation in which the mind's cherished beliefs and self-imposed limitations are challenged at every turn. The teacher's job is to push her students beyond the boundaries of what they think is possible, to up-end all notions of "I can't." For who is the "I" that can't, and what is "can't" but a construct of the mind? Dipa Ma had seen, through the development of her own powers, that there are no limits to what the mind can do. Sometimes she could be outrageous in her instructions and suggestions, at other times quietly and relentlessly persistent. She would walk her students right to the edge, and then urge them to go beyond. She also taught that "going beyond" could mean the simple willingness to reveal oneself, to let things unravel and come crashing down and, from that place, to keep on going.

The journey of transformation involves more, however, than the valiant effort to surpass one's limitations. It also requires us to balance our effort, our intentions, and our energy. Dipa Ma often said, "If you practice for a result, then it becomes a hindrance." The desire for liberation is nonetheless desire—

one of the key hindrances on the spiritual path. At one stage, zeal on the path is useful, and it moves us along; at another stage, this very thing that was so helpful becomes an impediment. We need to recognize when effort has become an obstruction. To stay with what is happening without giving up—sometimes that is all that is possible.

A fierce Burmese monk, U Pandita, frequently admonished his Western students to diligently "practice without regard for body or life." However, Howard Cohn points out that Dipa Ma's stance was slightly but significantly different: "Practice without regard for body or life—and with all the love in your heart." Dipa Ma perfected a mature form of effort, one that encompasses both strength and ease, the masculine and the feminine. Practice requires more than a zealous, samurai-warrior attitude. It also demands that we find compassion and love within ourselves. We can come to practice, like Dipa Ma, from a place of childlike wonder that is invincible in its truth and sincerity.

Steven Smith observed that "in Dipa Ma . . . there was a wondrous quality about making effort. Everything was an adventure; practicing through the middle of the night was an adventure. She embodied the realization that motivation for practice can come from the wonder of each moment."

"She taught me that mindfulness isn't something to strive for," echoes Sharon Kreider. "It's always there, it's going on all the time. Rather than something I have to seize, mindfulness is just being with what is, as it arises, all the time."

For many Western students, the greatest challenge can be to balance effort with ease, gentleness, and compassionate acceptance.

Practice all the time

❦ When Dipa Ma asked me about my practice, I told her that I meditated in the morning and the evening every day, and the rest of the day I worked at my job. Then she inquired, "Well, what do you do on weekends?" I don't remember my answer, but her response was, "There are two days. You should be practicing all day Saturday and Sunday." Then she gave me a strict lesson on how to optimize my time. I never forgot this lesson, this idea that I should be practicing all the time.

BOB RAY

Don't be lazy

❦ The last time I saw Dipa Ma before she died, she told me that I should sit for two days. She didn't mean a two-day retreat but one sitting two days long! I had to laugh; it seemed completely impossible. But with uncompromising compassion, she simply said to me, "Don't be lazy."

JOSEPH GOLDSTEIN

What are our limits?

❦ When Dipa Ma came to Insight Meditation Society to teach a three-month silent retreat in 1984, Joseph and Sharon were paired as a teaching team, and I was paired teaching with Dipa Ma. We would do interviews all morning, have lunch, and then Dipa Ma would go to her house across the street, and I would go to my room to rest before teaching again in the afternoon.

Just before I took my joyful little nap, I would look out my window and see Dipa Ma outside doing walking meditation. She was sick that year, and it was very cold; it would be snowing. She would have her white cotton sari on, walking back and forth in the snow. This from an old woman with a heart condition.

I would look out my window, and I'd look at Dipa Ma, and I'd look at my bed, and I'd look at Dipa Ma. . . . I felt I had to accept my limits. I knew I couldn't go outside and do walking meditation at that point, but I could appreciate and see the difference. Her unfailing dedication to really finish, to be fully liberated, made her so powerful, yet that power was utterly sweet. She never stopped. That, together with noticing that her actions didn't seem to reflect being motivated by aversion or attachment, was mind-boggling. I would see all this, and then I would go take a nap!

MICHELE MCDONALD

Only thoughts hold you back

In 1974, I stopped by Calcutta to say good-bye to Dipa Ma. I told her, "I'm going back to America for a short time to get my health together, to get some more money, and then I'll be back."

She shook her head and asserted, "No, when you go back to America you'll be teaching meditation with Joseph."

I said, "No, I won't," and she said, "Yes, you will," and I said, "No, I won't."

Finally, she just looked me in the eye and declared, "You can do anything you want to do. It's only your thought that you can't do it that's holding you back." She added, "You should teach because you really understand suffering."

This was a great blessing with which she sent me off, back to America. That was over thirty years ago. And she was right.

SHARON SALZBERG

You have enough time

❧ "If you are a householder, you have enough time," Dipa Ma told me. "Very early in the morning, you can take two hours for meditation. Late in the evening you can take another two hours for meditation. Learn to sleep only four hours. There is no need for sleeping more than four hours."

From that day on, I cut my sleeping time. I would meditate up until midnight sometimes, or get up early in the morning at two or three and meditate. Ma told us we had to stay healthy so we could continue practicing. She said observing the five precepts every day would keep me healthy.

PRITIMOYEE BARUA

Do whatever you can

❧ I asked Nani [Dipa Ma], "I heard you teach vipassana. What is that?"

She gave me an explanation of vipassana, then said, "I was once like you, suffering very much. I believe you can proceed in a way to become free."

I told her, "I have so many concerns with my mother and my son, and I also must run a family and a large bakery business. It is not possible for me to do this vipassana."

"Who says? When you are thinking about your son or mother, then think about them mindfully. When you are doing your household work, know that you are doing this. As a human being it is never possible to solve all your problems. The things you are facing and suffering, bring mindfulness to this."

"But between my bakery and my family, it is impossible to find even five minutes for meditation."

"If you can just manage five minutes a day, then do that. It is important to do whatever you can, no matter how little."

"I know I cannot spare five minutes. It is impossible."

Nani asked me if I would meditate with her, right then and there, for five minutes. So I sat with her for five minutes. She gave me instructions in meditation, even though I said I had no time.

Somehow I found five minutes a day, and I followed her instructions. And from this five minutes, I became so inspired. I did five minutes a day, and then more and more. Meditation became my first priority. I wanted to meditate whenever I could. I was able to find longer and longer times to meditate, and soon I was meditating many hours a day, into the night, sometimes all night after my work was done. I found energy and time I didn't know I had.

SUDIPTI BARUA

Pushed to the next level

❧ Almost every time I left Dipa Ma for more than a few hours, she would give me an exhortation to practice diligently. She was continually trying to push me to the next level: "I hope you will remember to sit X hours," or "I hope you will try to do X." Once or twice she used the words, "I expect you to. . . ." She always talked in a very soft voice, so it was never too intense, but underneath there was a real determination to it.

STEVEN SCHWARTZ

Continuous ease

❧ During my two-month retreat with Dipa Ma, her focus in our regular interviews was always on areas of my practice that needed work. For instance, what particular emotions were still strong? During what sitting or part of a sitting was concentration weak? How was I dealing with drowsiness at the end of the day? She didn't discourage enthusiasm about what was going well, but she always wanted to discuss what was inhibiting continuity in the practice.

What was fascinating about Dipa Ma was that she lived with that steadiness or continuity. It didn't matter if she was having lunch, going for a walk, or dealing with her young grandson, she did it with strong attention marked with a sense of ease.

I was reminded of Dipa Ma's approach to practice when we recently had a desert turtle living in our yard as a pet. The tightly woven fence never seemed to create an obstacle for this slow and steady creature. To keep track of him, we put a Band-Aid on his shell with our phone number on it. Days after each disappearance, the phone would ring and we would be awe-struck at how far and wide we would have to drive to retrieve him. When we placed him back in the yard, the moment his feet hit the ground he was beginning his next journey.

It was like that with Dipa Ma—one could see a profound continuity and effortlessness. She taught me that grace is really economy: not too much and not too little.

KATRINA SCHNEIDER

Are you really doing it?

She would always ask, "How much are you sitting. How is your mindfulness? How awake are you in your life?" Basically the question was, "Are you really doing it, or are you just thinking about it?" It's a great idea to live with mindfulness, but are you actually living your life that way?

JACK KORNFIELD

The dharma is everywhere

At the end of one retreat, I told Dipa Ma how hard it was to go back to my life because I was living in a remote part of the country where there wasn't a formalized sangha [community of practitioners]. I asked her about how to manage without a sangha and she said, "The dharma is everywhere. It doesn't matter where you are."

MICHELE MCDONALD

Impeccable effort

❀ Dipa Ma's greatest gift to me was showing me what was possible—and living it. She was impeccable about effort. People with this ability to make effort are not disheartened by how long it takes, how difficult it is. It takes months, it takes years, it doesn't matter, because the courage of the heart is there. She gave the sense that with right effort, anything is possible.

JOSEPH GOLDSTEIN

No excuses

❀ Dipa Ma was about no nonsense and no excuses. To say, "Oh, I'm too tired," or "The conditions aren't right," or "I have a backache, I don't want to practice today," there was no room for that. She made it clear that if you want to do it, you can do it if the commitment is there. For her, there was never a reason not to sit. She just didn't understand why we wouldn't always be practicing. Socializing was out of the question. Gossip and junk novels, no way!

CAROL WILSON

Mindful dreams

❀ Somebody asked her what her dreams were like and she said, "There is always mindfulness present in my dreams."

MICHAEL LIEBENSON GRADY

CHAPTER 5

SEEING THROUGH
OUR STORIES

"Let go of thinking, and your faith will come from within."

DIPA MA TAUGHT that the mind is all stories, one after another, like nesting dolls. You open one, and another is inside. Open that one, and there is another story emerging. When you get to the last nesting doll, the smallest one, and open it, inside of it is—what? It's empty, nothing there, and all around you are the empty shells of the stories of your life.

Because Dipa Ma was able literally to see through the stories of the mind, she did not acknowledge personal dramas of any kind. She wanted her students to live from a deeper truth than their interpretations of, and identification with, the external events of their lives. Dipa Ma knew all about life's dramas. She had personally suffered chronic illness; grief at the deaths of her parents, husband, and two children; and crushing despair. Only when she had gone beyond identification with the stories and dramas in her life did she begin to live as a free person.

No problem

Sometimes, when someone would come to her with their troubles, she would laugh and laugh.

She couldn't stop laughing. Finally she would say,
"This problem you are facing is no problem at all.
It is because you think, 'This is mine.' It is because
you think, 'There is something for me to solve.'
Don't think in this way, and then there will be no
trouble."

DIPAK CHOWDHURY

Don't think they are bowing to you

❧ When I was eight years old, I ordained as a
monk in Bodh Gaya at her suggestion. I was a monk
for three days. Immediately after I ordained, people began to bow to me. I thought, "Oh, wow!" I
felt very special. But my grandmother cautioned
me, "Don't think they are bowing to you. They are
bowing to your garments only."

RISHI BARUA (Dipa Ma's grandson)

Not special

❧ We were in the backseat of a car in Calcutta
one afternoon, going to visit Munindra. Dipa Ma
was sitting next to me and holding my hand.
Through her hand I could feel this incredible
tingly warmth of love in my body. I was basking in
it. It was for maybe a minute or two, and as I was
delighting in it, my mind jumped in with, "Oh,
you're special." The moment I had this thought,
she immediately but very gently let go of my hand
and didn't touch it again for the rest of the trip.

MATTHEW DANIELL

What is your intention?

❦ One night a student showed up who began asking Dipa Ma a lot of questions. He was quite challenging and confrontational and coming from an abstract intellectual place and trying to get her to argue. At one point she stopped and said in a very calm voice, "Why have you come here? What is your intention?" The sincerity of her question immediately silenced him.

AJAHN THANASANTI

Unraveling

❦ [Having just arrived in India] I wanted to see Ma right away. Jack, Joseph, and Sharon had said, "Just go!" So I went that evening at the first opportunity. I had her address, but I don't know how I found my way there. It was already getting dark by the time I arrived. I remember getting out of the taxi in this poor section of the city, and looking down this dark, dank alley with rubbish in it, and thinking, "I can't believe this is the right place." It was.

I pushed down the alley and came to a flight of open stairs on the right. I'd been told the fourth floor, but it was so hard to see, and I was getting more and more anxious, and I think I missed her floor the first time. I finally came out on the fourth-floor balcony and said her name to the first person I met. They pointed around the balcony to the other side of the open courtyard. By this time it must have been six or seven o'clock. Her students had gone for the day, and this was undoubtedly family

and personal time. I have to admit, with some
embarrassment, that I didn't think of this then. I
had just finished four months of intensive practice.
I had come all this way to study the dharma, and
I think I was more than a little self-preoccupied.

I saw a diminutive woman standing outside the
door and said something, and she motioned for me
to wait. She got her daughter, Dipa, to translate. I
introduced myself and explained that I was a dharma
student and friend of Joseph Goldstein and Sharon
Salzberg. She invited me into their small room.

I remember sitting on Ma's wooden bed and
starting to explain why I was there, and telling her
about all the intensive practice I had just done and
what I'd experienced. She couldn't have been
kinder or more welcoming. She listened patiently
and attentively as Dipa translated, as though she
had nothing better to do at that moment than listen to this young man who had just intruded into
her home and was full of his experiences. As I continued to talk, something in me started to unravel.

It's never happened to me before or since like
it did that evening. I've certainly been anxious meeting people before; I've met many other people of
note in various walks of life over the years. But nothing like this. The more I talked, the more a tide of
panic and confusion rose up and overwhelmed me.
My mind started spinning wildly out of control. I
think I must have started making no sense whatso-
ever. I felt completely and utterly abashed. All my

grandiosity, all my self-importance, all my experiences, all my sense of specialness and being on this extraordinary spiritual pilgrimage just came crashing down around my ears in a matter of minutes. And Ma hadn't done anything other than sit there and hold me gently in her gaze and her attention.

JACK ENGLER

Everything is impermanent

When my son died in 1984, Dipa Ma shocked me with her words. It was a hard teaching I have not forgotten: "Today your son has gone from this world. Why are you shocked? Everything is impermanent. Your life is impermanent. Your husband is impermanent. Your son is impermanent. Your daughter is impermanent. Your money is impermanent. Your building is impermanent. Everything is impermanent. There is nothing that is permanent. When you are alive, you might think, 'This is my daughter, this is my husband, this is my property, this is my building, this car belongs to me.' But when you are dead, nothing is yours. Sudipti, you think you are a serious meditator, but you must really learn that everything is impermanent."

SUDIPTI BARUA

Without the worry

Everything that I feared most—losing my husband, losing my children—had happened to Dipa Ma, and yet here she was, tranquil and equanimous and cheerful. To see her with the same causes for concern as I had, but without the worry, was inspirational.

SYLVIA BOORSTEIN

Letting go

A number of Americans, concerned about the poor conditions in Dipa Ma's neighborhood, collected donations to help her move away from the inner city. One student recalled what happened when he delivered the money to build the new house.

Altogether I had about twenty-five hundred dollars for this house fund, which I figured in Indian money was enough to build half of a house. It was more than Dipa Ma's family had to live on for a year. Because I loved her so much—and probably also because I was feeling some self-importance—I took the responsibility for delivering this money quite seriously, but also with a lot of delight.

"Wait until she sees what I'm bringing her," I thought. "One half of a house!"

When I got there, I told her I had brought some money in American dollars. She said, "We can't change American dollars. We are not even allowed to have dollars. You should convert them into rupees." The exchange rate being what it was at the time, twenty-five hundred dollars was worth around forty-five thousand rupees. I went to the American Express Bank, and the largest denomination they had was a hundred-rupee note. I walked out of the place with my backpack stuffed full of rupees.

I had been ripped off twice in India—once for a thousand dollars—so I was nervous carrying this sum of money in cash through the streets of Calcutta. I felt like I was carrying Dipa Ma's future on my back: her house, her entire worldly fortune, and her chance for a life of comfort. I went straight from the bank to her apartment. It took about an hour to travel there, and every step of the way I was in a state of high anxiety. But I couldn't wait to see her face. We thought it would take five years to raise the money, and here, within the first three months, I was to deliver half the house to her. "She will be so happy," I thought.

By the time I got to the apartment, I was literally sweating. As I walked in the door, Dipa Ma put her hands on my head and gave me her usual blessing. "You look quite distraught," she said. I didn't want to say, "Well, I'm basically afraid of the people in your country. I thought I'd be ripped off." Instead, I just said, "Well, I had to go change the money. It was really quite a lot of money, and I was concerned about having so much cash on me."

I took off my pack, opened it, and emptied it out onto the floor. The place suddenly looked like a scene in a movie, with piles and piles of rupees all over the apartment. Dipa Ma didn't blink an eye. She didn't even move or offer any expression of enthusiasm or excitement. She just took the money, slid it under her bed, and covered it up with a piece of cloth.

I thought, "Under the bed? Forty-five thousand rupees—you don't want to stash that sum of money under your bed. Let's put the money some-place where it won't get stolen. And what about your new house? Let's talk about your house."

She said nothing about the money or the house. Instead, she was only concerned about me. She said, "You should quiet down. Don't be nerv-ous." Then she turned to Dipa and said, "We need to feed him."

On my way out I thought maybe I'd better men-tion the money to Dipa. "Your mother put all this money under the bed." I said. "I'm concerned it might not be safe. You should take it to the bank."

Dipa laughed. "Oh, it would not be safe in the bank. But it will be safe here."

I started to protest, but then I realized that the problem from the very beginning was me. I was not simply being a vehicle for other people's generosity. I had taken this on as "mine." I had turned it into a big deal by infusing my sense of self-importance into the situation. Even after I had turned the money over to them, I hadn't been too willing to let it go. But when Dipa said, "Don't worry, it will be safe," I was finally able to say, "Okay, it's yours."

I never asked another question or had a sec-ond thought about the money or the house. When I walked out of their apartment, I felt free of that burden. In fact, I never even learned whether they actually built the house. And this is the first time I've thought about it in almost twenty years.

STEVEN SCHWARTZ

Why be upset?

❧ When she stood up against something she felt was wrong, sometimes others would blame and criticize her. But she was not bothered by this. She told me, "Why be upset? Even the Buddha had to bear slanders and criticism throughout his life, and I am just an ordinary and insignificant woman!"

DIPA BARUA

The dharma is very special

❧ His Holiness the 16th Karmapa, the head of one of the great lineages of Tibetan Buddhism, visited IMS one year when Dipa Ma was teaching there. All the yogis and teachers were going up to him for blessings, and he would tap them on the head with a ritual object. When Dipa Ma went up to him, he took her head between both his hands and spoke softly with her. It was clear that there was some recognition going on between them, even though they had never met before.

In the tradition of Tibetan Buddhism, there was elaborate preparation for the Karmapa's visit. A teaching throne was built and covered with beautiful brocade. Some people were wondering about all these preparations, which were in stark contrast to Dipa Ma's utter simplicity. When they asked her about it, she said, "Oh, he does that so people will see the dharma as being very special."

JOSEPH GOLDSTEIN

CHAPTER 6

THE DEEPEST FREEDOM

"Gradually I became acquainted with suffering, the cause of suffering, the arising of suffering, and the end of suffering."

DIPA MA BELIEVED, unconditionally, that enlightenment—total liberation of the mind and heart—is the purpose of human life and the primary reason for meditation practice. She never tired of reminding her students: "You must practice to know at least one stage of enlightenment. Otherwise you have not made use of your human life."

In the Theravada tradition, little is written about the actual experience of enlightenment. The reticence of many teachers on this subject is largely to avoid setting up an attitude of striving. This chapter brings enlightenment experiences out into the open, with the aim of showing that there is nothing secret or supernatural about them. Although it might be inferred from these stories that enlightenment can happen rather easily, there are also stories of awakening taking many years or even decades.

While there is no "right way" on this path, and consequently nothing to judge, compare, or anticipate, Joseph Goldstein offers this important caveat: "The experience of enlightenment is about letting go of 'self.' Over the years, I've seen people who have experienced enlightenment use it to create more self. They attach to the experience and identify with it. This is missing the point, and it can create a lot of suffering."

Kamikaze yogi

My first two three-month retreats were blasting through, "bliss bomb"–type retreats, where I described myself as a kamikaze yogi. But my third three-month retreat was weeping from the first day until the end. At times, I would have such incredible internal aching and tearing apart that I thought I couldn't sit more than five minutes. At first, when I reported this to Dipa Ma, she suggested I just "note it."

But finally there was a certain point where I really thought I was going to explode if I sat any longer. Dipa Ma sat down next to me, took my hand, held it and caressed it with love and gentleness, like caressing a baby. While she was doing this, she assured me, "If you make it through this, you will earn great merit."

Doing this, she gave me an absolute transmission of her confidence and love. My doubt disappeared; I totally believed her words. I went back to the hall and sat on my cushion, and . . . something just opened up. I don't know how much I should describe of it. I started to have experiences like you see in the classical texts on enlightenment. She was guiding me with special resolutions during this time.

I am grateful that she kept me practicing. Even though for two and a half months I was racked with restlessness and achiness and wanted to "roll up the mat" and go home, she kept me going.

ANONYMOUS

Did you get enlightened?

Dipa Ma came to teach a class at my school for three weeks. At the end of the class, we were to do a weekend intensive retreat with her. The day before the intensive she said to me, "You are going to have a 'realization experience'." I wondered, "What is this supposed to mean?"

That night, I meditated for a while, and then I got up because I was getting very sleepy. I went back to my room, and something shifted. I realized I needed to go back and meditate some more, so I went back to meditate, and I got extremely concentrated. There was simply the watching of my breath. I was noting every microcosm of the rising and falling, every little bit, and I had the ability to watch the intentions of thoughts coming. It was like a bubble that would break, then the thought would be there, then it would pass, and there would be stillness, then another intention of the thought would arise, then break like a bubble on the surface of water and so on.

It was not me doing this, because I absolutely had no capacity for that level of concentration. I think it was simply by Dipa Ma's grace. There was incredible stillness, and a huge amount of space in between thoughts where nothing was going on.

Then there was a huge shift in awareness, as if I went "out" somewhere where attention reversed. There was no body anymore, just the arising and passing away of things. It completely blew me away.

The next day Dipa Ma asked me, "Well, did you get enlightened?" Later, because I was so new at meditation—I didn't have a background or context for this experience—a lot of fear came up. First there was this incredible insight, then fear arose when I saw that everything was being annihilated moment after moment. My mind became so confused; I didn't have the ability to watch the confusion, and it was a long time before the experience matured in me. It was three years before I had the desire to meditate again.

ANONYMOUS

Enlightenment was rather matter-of-fact to Dipa Ma's Indian students. Jack Engler recalls that they practiced within the context of their families and daily life. "When Dipa Ma recognized a certain kind of ripeness in them, she would say, 'Arrange your affairs, see if you can get two weeks off from the family, and come and stay in this room next to me and just devote yourself for ten or fourteen days to this practice.' That's when enlightenment happened to them. That is all the intensive practice they did, and even then, some of them had to return home during that time to take care of family matters."

Just two or three days

❧I took my mother [Dipa Ma's sister Hema] every evening to the monastery, and once I met a

Burmese lady there who told me about her practice at home with her small children. She worked
in the day, and she did meditation at night when
her children were asleep. Within two months, she
said, she finished the first stage [of enlightenment].

So I took that example while I was teaching full
time and studying in my master's program. I got
up at 4 AM and meditated until 5:30 AM. I went to
school until 3:30 PM, then I took my mother to the
monastery. After that I would do my homework
until 9 PM. Then I would do walking meditation
for an hour with my dog. Then I would sit for
another hour until 11 PM. At 11, I went to sleep.

All the time, on the bus to school, during my
classes, everywhere, I practiced noting [mentally
noting each sensory experience]. After about two
or three weeks, Munindra told me to take my vaca-
tion and come and meditate. I told him it was
impossible to take time off school, and he said,
"Well, just two or three days will do." So I went
for Thursday through Sunday. Since there was so
little time, I decided to stay up all night Thursday,
and I kept meditating into Friday.

On Friday night at about 1 AM, I thought something "went wrong." In the morning, I told my
mother and Dipa Ma that something strange had
happened. They started laughing and laughing. They
told me it was the first stage, and they were very
glad for me.

DAW THAN MYINT

Okay, a tiger is coming

❧ On the very first day I met her, Nani [Dipa Ma] gave me meditation instructions and told me, "You can practice at home." I went home that afternoon and immediately started practicing for twenty days.

During the twenty days of meditation, I felt I had a high fever, I felt like a hot iron was penetrating my body. Then I saw snakes everywhere, and tigers were jumping at me. I reported this to Nani, and she told me, "Don't worry. Don't take any medicine. You have a fever, but it is not a disease: it will spontaneously leave. Just be mindful of it. Just feel it and note it. When snakes or tigers come, don't worry. Just notice, 'Okay, a tiger is coming.' That is all."

Then I began having vivid pictures of dead bodies. I saw many, many dead bodies in an arid place, and I had to walk on the dead bodies. I was terrified. Nani said, "Don't fear. Just make a mental note of 'seeing.' These visions are from our many births. What we have done in previous births often comes to mind in meditation." From her instruction, I noted, "seeing a dead body," and "walking on dead bodies." I also kept noting, "I'm seeing in my mind."

Soon there was just awareness, everything stopped, my mind became clear and peaceful, and I came to awaken. All my pains were eradicated. I came to understand what was my body, what was my mind, and what was the way of meditation.

There was no turning back. After twenty days, I left
my seat and went out into the world.

JYOTISHMOYEE BARUA

This most precious thing

When I was doing my research in Calcutta,
Dipa Ma brought her neighbor to me, a sixty-five-
year-old woman whose name was Madhuri Lata.
She had raised her family, her children were gone,
and, unlike most Indian families, she was alone with
her husband, with no extended family living in the
same household. Her husband had said to her, "You
have nothing to do now. This 'aunt' of yours, Dipa
Ma, teaches this meditation practice. Why don't
you talk with her? It'll give you something to do."

Madhuri, who had mild developmental delays,
went to Dipa Ma, and Dipa Ma gave her the basic
instructions [to place her attention on the rise and
fall of the abdomen with each inhalation and exha-
lation and] to note to herself "rising, falling, rising,
falling." Madhuri said, "Okay," and started to go
home, down four flights of stairs and across the
alley to her apartment. She didn't get halfway down
the stairs before she forgot the instructions. So, back
she came.

"What was I supposed to do?" she asked.

"Rising, falling, rising, falling," said Dipa Ma.

"Oh, yes, that's right."

Four times, Madhuri forgot the instructions and
had to come back. Dipa Ma was very patient with
her. It took Madhuri almost a year to understand

the basic instructions, but once she got them, she was like a tiger. Before she began to practice, Madhuri was bent over at a ninety-degree angle with arthritis, rheumatism, and intestinal problems. When I met her, after her enlightenment experience, she walked with a straight back. No more intestinal problems. She was the simplest, sweetest, gentlest woman.

After she told me her enlightenment story, she said, "All this time, I've wanted to tell someone about this wonderful thing that happened to me, and I've never been able to share this before, this most precious thing in my life."

JACK ENGLER

All emotion is from thinking

Despite severe emotional difficulties, a Vietnamese monk, Venerable Khippa-Panno, was able to attain insight with Dipa Ma's encouragement. In 1969, he had gone on a retreat during which, for five days, he was unable to stop laughing and crying. His teacher, deciding Khippa-Panno had gone mad, told him to stop the retreat and return home. When Dipa Ma heard this, she invited Khippa-Panno to practice with her.

For a whole month, I practiced at her house. She advised me, "You will overcome this difficulty. If everything is noted, all your emotional difficulties will disappear. When you feel happy, don't get involved with the happiness. And when you feel sad, don't get involved with it. Whatever comes, don't worry. Just be aware of it."

On a later retreat, when I felt the craziness come, I remembered her words. I had so much difficulty with the emotions that I wanted to leave the retreat, but I remembered her faith in me, and her saying, "Your practice is good. Just note everything, and you will overcome the difficulty." With this knowledge of her confidence in me, my concentration got deeper.

Soon I came to see that all emotion was from thinking, nothing more. I found that once I knew how to observe the thoughts that led to the emotions, I could overcome them. And then I came to see that all thoughts were from the past or the future, so I started to live only in the present, and I developed more and more mindfulness. . . . I had no thoughts for a period of time, just mindfulness, and then all my emotional difficulties passed away. Just like that! And then I had an experience. I wasn't sure what it was. It was only a moment, and there wasn't anyone to confirm it at the time. My emotional problems have never returned.

Later, in 1984, when I saw Dipa Ma in America, she took me aside and asked about my meditation. When I told her, she told me that I had completed the first stage [of enlightenment]. She told me like a mother would tell a child.

VENERABLE KHIPPA-PANNO

CHAPTER 7

HOW ARE YOU LIVING YOUR LIFE?

"The whole path of mindfulness is this:
Whatever you are doing,
be aware of it."

THE PARTNER OF a spiritual teacher once said, "I know he's learning something because he's less difficult to live with." Insights that are genuine change our whole way of being; they make us gentler with each other and with the planet. Perhaps your practice has rewarded you with deep insights. But wonderful as they are, such experiences are fleeting. Enlightened or not, the question remains: How are you living your life? It's a simple test, but an important one: How do you wash the dishes? How do you react when someone cuts you off on the freeway?

Dipa Ma was a living example of how to live in this world, of how practice and the mundane activities of our day-to-day existence can be made one. She insisted that the practice be done all the time, and that we do the things we do throughout the day without making them into problems. Dipa Ma wanted to know, "How awake are you in your life? Are you just thinking about being mindful, or are you really doing it?"

Dipa Ma said that even while she was talking, she was meditating. Talking, eating, working, thinking about her daughter, playing with her grandson—none of those activities hampered her practice because she did them all with mindfulness. "When I'm moving, shopping, everything, I'm always doing it with mindfulness. I know these are things I have to do, but they aren't problems. On the other hand, I don't spend time gossiping or visiting or doing anything which I don't consider necessary in my life."

How do you tie your shoes?

She encouraged me to live what I was teaching. The quality of her presence was like that in the Hasidic tales, where somebody asked, "Why did you go to see this rabbi? Did you go to hear him give a great lecture on the Torah, or see how he worked with his students?" And the person said, "No, I went to see how he tied his shoes." Dipa Ma didn't want people to come and live in India forever or be monks or join an ashram. She said, "Live your life. Do the dishes. Do the laundry. Take your kids to kindergarten. Raise your children or your grandchildren. Take care of the community in which you live. Make all of that your path, and follow your path with heart."

JACK KORNFIELD

Enlightened ironing

She believed you could become enlightened ironing your clothes. . . . She felt that every activity should be given that much mindfulness. And the care should be there, too—care for whoever you were ironing the clothes for.

MICHELLE LEVEY

Laundry with saint

❀My favorite scene in all the [8-mm home movie] footage I shot of Dipa Ma is of her hanging out the laundry. Remember that Zen saying, "After the ecstasy, the laundry"? Well, there is this long shot, maybe two or three minutes of Dipa  Ma smiling and enjoying hanging out the laundry. It's wonderful to see her in the sunshine, in the yard. I would like to take a frame of this and call it "Laundry with Saint."

JACK KORNFIELD

The sacred within the mundane

❀When I knocked on the door, Ma's daughter Dipa answered. I was quite excited about meeting Dipa Ma and had a bundle of questions I wanted to ask her about meditation. After a few minutes an elderly woman [Dipa Ma] appeared. She seemed totally uninterested in my presence. She didn't look at me; she didn't acknowledge me. She was so incredibly silent and quiet, so grounded and present, that I knew I would have to wait until she was ready to relate to me. It wasn't aloofness, exactly. Rather it was a sense of real stillness.

When she came into the room, she picked up
a little plastic toy duck that must have belonged
to her grandchild and took it over to a plastic basin
on the windowsill. In the soft afternoon light coming through the window, she began bathing the
duck. It was like baptizing this little plastic toy. What
impressed me most was that she did it so wholeheartedly. Here were these objects that were so mundane, in some sense the opposite of spiritual, just
a dirty old plastic toy, yet she did the whole process
so wholeheartedly. It immediately centered me just
watching her.

ANDREW GETZ

Impeccable morality

❧ When fall began to turn into winter at IMS,
my role was to round up the appropriate winter
clothes for Dipa Ma's family. Someone made Dipa
Ma a shawl, and others began contributing cloth-
ing. One of the items I gave her was a very
comfortable pair of warm socks, which she wore
regularly around the house. I was pleased that my
small gift was proving so useful to her. But I made
the careless mistake, in all the busyness of those
days, of having brought them to her without for-
mally offering them as a gift.

After seven weeks of sharing day-to-day life, the
time came for me to take Dipa Ma and her family
to the airport and to say good-bye. When I came
back to the house, I was filled with sadness. A period
of great intensity was over. The house felt so empty.

When I went into her bedroom, I found a few items neatly placed on the foot of her bed. One of them was the pair of socks. My heart sank. I couldn't understand why she had consciously left them behind.

After some reflection, I realized that the socks were given in an unclear way, that she would not assume that they were hers to keep. As small as this incident seems, it held a powerful teaching in what impeccable sila [morality] looks like—a lesson which was painful at the time, but one that I would remember.

MICHAEL LIEBENSON GRADY

Relentlessly present

I asked Dipa Ma, "Would you like to move into the other room to sit? There is a group coming over this evening."

"I'm sitting now. Why go to the other room to sit?"

"Well, we're going to do a little sitting in there."

"We are sitting."

"But other people want to come, and they'll be sitting in the other room."

Finally I got her to go into the other room and sit. She could just "be there," relentlessly. Her eyes could be open, her eyes could be closed, it really didn't make any difference. That was the most remarkable aspect of her presence in our house, the sense of, "Why move? What is there really to do?"

At these sittings, sometimes fifty people might arrive to receive her blessings, but no matter how many came she would take each person one by one and be completely present. In watching the singularity of her focus and connectedness, I could see she was relating to each person as God.

STEVEN SCHWARTZ

Just standing, just sitting

❧ I never ever saw Dipa Ma have a restless or distracted moment, and I used to watch her all the time. When she would stand, it was like a rock dropping. She would just stand. And when she sat, she sat. Period. There was never anything else going on. She didn't look around or ever lose her focus.

MICHAEL LIEBENSON GRADY

Beeline to the Buddha

❧ In Calcutta, a student of Dipa Ma's and Munindra's who had become financially successful held a big celebration to bless a new house. I walked up the stairs with Dipa Ma and helped her with her shoes. People were talking and eating, the stereo was on, and the buoyancy in the atmosphere was like a champagne party. The room was charged with an excited, loud energy.

Dipa Ma walked in the door and in her steady, even-paced way, immediately made a beeline to the Buddha [across the room]. When she was in front of the image, she got down on the floor and began bowing, right in the middle of everyone eating hors

d'oeuvres and celebrating. I realized that for Dipa
Ma, no matter what was happening, she had only
one aim, and that was the truth.

AJAHN THANASANTI

You just do it

❧ Speaking to me as a teacher she would ask,
"What are your sittings like? Do you practice? Do
you have any thoughts?"

"What do you mean *any* thoughts? Millions of
thoughts," I would think.

"Stop them."

"What do you mean, stop them? I can, with
great yogic effort, but it takes me a long time to
build up the samadhi."

"No," she would simply say, "you sit down and
you just do it."

JACK KORNFIELD

It's okay

❧ When I was on my way from Bangkok to
Delhi, my plane had a technical problem and needed
to land in Calcutta. I had a twenty-four-hour lay-
over, and I thought, "This would be a nice way to
meet Dipa Ma." I found out where she lived and
went to her apartment. When I arrived, I was told
she was on a silent retreat and I wouldn't be able
to talk to her. I was told to only go in her room,
do my bows and leave. When I went into her room
it happened that she was eating and had her back
to me. In the room there was this incredible energy,

of calm and softness and it brought a wave of emotion and tears for me. She could not see me because I was standing behind her, but she must have felt me, because she turned around and said to me very softly, "It's okay. It's okay." That is all she said, but it was so peaceful and calming. She met my heart when it needed it in a very beautiful and spontaneous way. That moment has stayed with me. In times of great difficulty I remember her simply saying, "It's okay." She showed me that everything is okay and that it's all part of our path.

PATRICIA GENOUD-FELDMAN

LOVE
BOWING TO LOVE

"Your heart knows everything."

IN A BUSY Santa Fe coffeehouse one morning, Sharon Salzberg was asked, "What was Dipa Ma's greatest gift to you?"

Sharon paused for a moment, and her face softened.

"Dipa Ma really loved me," she said. "And when she died, I wondered, 'Will anyone ever really love me like that again?'"

She fell silent, and for a few moments it was as if a gate had opened into another world. In this other place there was only one thing: complete and total love.

"Of course," Sharon added with a quiet smile, "it wasn't just me. It wasn't personal."

Jacqueline Mandell once asked Dipa Ma whether she should be practicing mindfulness or lovingkindness. Dipa Ma answered, "From my own experience, there is no difference between mindfulness and lovingkindness." For her, love and awareness were one. Think about it. When you are fully loving, aren't you also mindful? When you are fully mindful, is this not also the essence of love?

Joseph Goldstein recalls that once when he saw Dipa Ma bow to the Buddha, it was so clear that there was no one there, it was just "love bowing to love." Another student said, "To Dipa Ma, enlightenment was great love. Her teachings were about connecting to others and being kind." Her heart, like the door to her apartment, was always open. And in that great heart, everyone—whether in sorrow or in celebration—could come and go and be held in her loving embrace. A Sufi teacher, Asha Greer, described being hugged by Dipa Ma "so thoroughly that my six feet fit into her great vast empty heart, with room for the whole of creation."

Blessing for a thief

For a couple of years, it seemed that whenever I visited New York City, my car would get broken into and my radio ripped off. I'd been invited to a friend's wedding in Queens. I told Dipa Ma that I was thinking of taking the train because my radio always gets stolen.

"Don't be silly," she said. "Go by car."

So we ended up taking the car, which by that time had a security system installed in it. We parked the car and went to the wedding. When we came out, sure enough, my car had been broken into yet again. This time they took not only the radio but all my tapes, too.

When we got back, I walked into the house, and Dipa Ma asked, "How was the wedding?"

"The wedding was great," I said. "But my car got broken into again, and the radio was stolen. I'm really upset."

Dipa Ma just burst out laughing.

"What's so funny?"

"You must have been a thief in your former lifetime. How many more times do you think you will need to have your radio stolen?"

"You tell me," I demanded. "How many more times? Tell me, so I can be prepared."

Ignoring my question, she asked, "What did you do? What was your reaction when the car was broken into?"

"I was really angry because it's happened so many times. And I thought I had a security system."

She looked at me in amazement. "You mean you didn't even think about the man who took your radio, how sad his life must be?"

She closed her eyes and started chanting quietly to herself, and I knew she was saying metta [lovingkindness blessings] for the thief. It was a wonderful lesson for me.

Steven Schwartz

Another person to love

She was very loving and very grandmotherly. When you would come in, especially in India, her first questions were, "How are you feeling? How is your health? Are you eating well, are you doing okay with our climate and food?" and so forth. . . . She would smile when people walked in the room, and there was this outpouring of welcoming lovingkindness. It didn't matter who came in, or what circumstances, or what they had to say: that level

was irrelevant to her. What was important was simply that here was another person to be loved.

JACK KORNFIELD

I have a gift for you, too

❧ On my first trip to India, my friend Sharon Salzberg accompanied me and shared some of her favorite experiences with me. In Benares there was a particular sweet that she wanted me to try called rasmali. It was delicious.

Back in Calcutta we went to see Dipa Ma, who asked me, "What was your favorite thing in India?" I imagine the right answer would have been something like, "I prayed in a temple in Bodh Gaya," or "I saw a wonderful picture of the Buddha," or "I went on retreat." But instead, I blurted out the first thing that came into my head, which was, "I had these sweets in Benares, and they were so good." Sharon gave me a look, and I wondered how Dipa Ma felt about my answer.

Later, leaving Calcutta, we stopped by her house to pay respects on our way to the airport. We bowed and offered her a gift. "I have a gift for you, too," she said, setting some rasmali sweets before us.

She had sent a friend of Dipa's searching all over Calcutta to find the sweet I had tasted in Benares. I was so moved by this act of giving me anything I wanted, whatever it was. If I said I enjoyed it, she would feed that part of me.

STEVEN SCHWARTZ

Lovingkindness for your mother

🪷 I met a man who had practiced in India in the late 1960s and early '70s. He was an avid meditator. He shaved his head, he wore white, he spent years in temples and ashrams and monasteries. His parents hated it. He was probably in his early thirties at the time, and his parents thought he should be in medical school or law school. His mother was particularly unhappy. It was as if he had died, as if she had lost a son.

Whenever he went to see Dipa Ma, she would ask him about his mother. "How is your mother? How is she doing? When you do your sittings, are you doing metta for your mother? Every time you sit, you should put your mother in your heart and send her lovingkindness."

One time she reached under the mattress in her back room and pulled out a roll of Indian bank notes. She took out a hundred-rupee note, worth about twelve dollars, which was a lot of money for her. She put it in his hand, closed his fingers over it, and said, "Go buy a present and send it to your mother." That was how she taught.

JACK KORNFIELD

Strokes for all

🪷 When Dipa Ma first got to our New England house, she and Rishi were nervous about the dog. She had never lived in a house where the dog stayed inside. Dogs in her Calcutta neighborhood were generally unhealthy, so having dogs in the house just didn't make sense.

Over a couple of weeks, though, this wonderful transformation happened between her and the dog. "Dog" was the first English word that she learned. Every morning she would come downstairs and say in halting English, "Dog, where is dog?" And our dog Yeats would come running over, and she would get down on her knees and stroke him with lovingkindness, just like she stroked me and the other meditators.

Yeats really appreciated this. It was very beautiful to watch the two of them connect, in part because she was nervous at the outset; you could see that there was this conditioning that was part of her culture. But she just took him into her heart, and they became great friends. The day she left, she went over to Yeats and got down and talked to him and gave him a special lovingkindness prayer.

STEVEN SCHWARTZ

Anagarika Teddy

While Dipa Ma was at IMS in 1984, I spotted a big teddy bear sitting atop the trash to be picked up in the neighborhood. I rescued it and gave it to Dipa Ma's grandson Rishi, who was also here with his mom. We named the bear Anagarika Teddy [one meaning for "anagarika" is literally "homeless one"]. When Dipa and family left IMS, Teddy remained in my care, and I more or less forgot about him.

A couple years later, I went to India and visited Dipa Ma in Calcutta. When she saw me, she immediately asked, "How is Anagarika Teddy?" She had not forgotten even a teddy bear saved from the trash. I was taken aback. It made me realize how much she must also care for living, breathing beings like myself. It revealed to me her clarity of mind as well.

Buzz Bussewitz

When the heart is not afraid

When Dipa Ma was about to leave the Insight Meditation Society, a whole group of us, twenty or so, were standing near her, holding our hands together at our hearts. For some reason, just before she got in the van, she turned to me and put her hands on my hands, looked me right in the eye, remarkably close, and held my hands in silence. She stared at me with utter love, utter emptiness, utter care. During this minute she gave me a complete, heartfelt transmission of lovingkindness . . . there was shakti [spiritual energy] just pouring from her. Then she turned around and slowly got into the car.

In this one moment, she showed me a kind of love I had never experienced before. It was a rare kind of love without separation or differences. This was my first taste of what can happen in the presence of an enlightened being. That moment is just as powerful as if it had happened yesterday.

Knowing this love, and seeing that it's possible to give it to others, has been a real inspiration for me on my path. Dipa Ma is an example of how, when the heart is not afraid, the love can just pour through

SHARDA ROGELL

This life is in trouble

There was a period in my life when I was deeply unhappy. My marriage was on the rocks, and I was ashamed of my lack of patience as a mother. Ironically, it was a time when, to the outside world, my life looked fine and successful: I should have been happy. I was talking to Jack Kornfield about my struggle. He mentioned that there was a wonderful woman teacher that he met in India who was visiting nearby at Sylvia Boorstein's house.

When I arrived at Sylvia's I was shown up to the attic room. Dipa Ma was seated on a zafu and her translator was sitting to her left. I began to settle myself on the cushion in front of her. Before I could even drop into a position of stillness, she turned to the interpreter and said something in Bengali. He said to me, "She says don't even bother to do vipassana right now; do only metta (lovingkindness)." I was startled. We hadn't greeted each other and usually the student asks a question before the teacher responds. "Why?" I asked. Again, she said something in Bengali, and the interpreter translated, "Your 'this life' is in trouble, and you need to work on it now, so do only metta." He then motioned that the interview was at an end. I was stunned. The entire interaction had taken less than two minutes. I knew that the term "this life" meant my feelings toward myself. Clearly she had seen my unhappiness, and the antidote she had prescribed was lovingkindness.

My meeting with Dipa Ma inspired me, and even though I found it quite difficult, I worked with the metta, reciting the phrases inwardly many times a day and throughout my sitting practice. At first, I couldn't feel a positive response, but I continued. It took about three months before I could begin to feel some genuine warmth toward myself. At the end of six months, I could feel a definite shift in myself when I would bring my attention to the practice. I could feel more softness, openness, and even affection. Somehow Dipa Ma found just the right way to wake me up, give me a tool to change my thinking pattern, and create a major shift in my life.

WENDY PALMER

CHAPTER 9

AT HOME
IN STRANGE REALMS

*"1 went back mind-moment
by mind-moment."*

DIPA MA DEVELOPED her supernatural powers under Munindra's tutelage and never demonstrated them except at his request. Such powers are achieved not through insight meditation, but through concentration practices, in which the mind enters a deep state of absorption known as a jhana. While she was doing jhana practice, Dipa Ma could enter any of the eight classical jhanic states at will and stay in it as long as she wanted. In the deeper jhanas, bodily processes can sometimes slow almost to a standstill, so it is not necessary to drink, eat, sleep, move, or urinate. Dipa Ma could resolve to enter a specific jhana and "wake up" or emerge from it at a predetermined time. On one occasion, she resolved to enter the eighth jhana and stay in it for three days, twenty-one hours, eight minutes, and three seconds. She emerged from the jhana exactly to the second that she had predetermined.

When she left Burma, Dipa Ma stopped practicing these powers, insisting that they involve ego and are therefore a hindrance to liberation. Munindra concurred. "These powers are not important," he said. "Enlightenment is important.

You need wisdom to use these powers. You don't want to use these powers with ego, because they are not yours. You can't use them and think you're the one who is powerful. This is not wisdom."

Jack Engler once asked Dipa Ma if she still possessed the extraordinary powers she had acquired years before while studying with Munindra.

"No," she said.

"Could you get them back?"

"Yes," she said, "but it would take a long time."

"How long?" asked Jack, thinking she would reply in terms of months or years.

"Oh, about three days," she replied, "if I really practiced."

There are said to be six higher powers: five mundane powers, accessed through the extraordinary degree of concentration in the fourth jhana, and one supramundane power, attainable only through insight practice and considered a mark of full enlightenment. The five mundane powers are found in all the shamanic and yogic traditions, and occur spontaneously to a lesser extent in some individuals. They are said to be:

Supernatural powers: the ability to transform one of the four basic elements of the physical world (earth, air, fire, and water) into another.

Divine ear: the ability to hear sounds near and far, on earth and in other realms.

Divine eye: The ability to see into the future, to see things near and far, on earth and in other realms.

Knowledge of one's former births and the previous births of others.

Knowledge of the states of mind of other beings; that is, the ability to "read" or know the minds of others.

According to Munindra, Dipa Ma demonstrated each of these powers to him. The following accounts are based on Munindra's recollections. "You may not believe it," he said, "but it's true."

Once Munindra was in his room when he noticed something unusual in the sky outside his window. He looked out and saw Dipa Ma in the air near the tops of the trees, grinning at him and playing in a room she had built in the sky. By changing the air element into the earth element, she had been able to create a structure in mid-air.

Changing denser elements to air produced only slightly less astonishing occurrences. Sometimes Dipa Ma and her sister Hema arrived for interviews with Munindra by spontaneously appearing in his room, and Dipa Ma occasionally left by walking through the closed door. If she was feeling especially playful, she might rise from her chair, go to the nearest wall, and walk right through it.

Dipa Ma learned to cook food by making the fire element come out of her hands. She could also change the earth element into the water element, which she demonstrated to Munindra by diving into a patch of ground and emerging with her clothes and hair wet. If she had to walk alone at night, Dipa Ma could duplicate her body, creating a companion for herself so that no one would bother her.

Dipa Ma's abilities in this regard were once tested by a third party. Munindra knew a professor of Ancient Indian History at Magadh University who was skeptical about psychic powers. Munindra offered to prove the existence of such powers, and the two of them set up an experiment. The professor posted a trusted graduate student in a room where Dipa Ma was meditating to watch and make sure she didn't leave the room. On the appointed day, the student verified that Dipa Ma never left her meditation posture, and yet, at the very same time, she appeared at the professor's office ten miles away and had a conversation with him.

Dipa Ma and Hema once used their extraordinary powers in tandem to move a bus. One afternoon in Rangoon, they were waiting at a bus stop. When the bus finally arrived, over an hour late, they realized they were going to miss their engagement some distance away. Because it was important to arrive on time, they both began to concentrate and got the bus back on schedule. "During the samadhi [absorptive] state," Munindra explained, "they made resolutions and moved the bus even while sitting in it. They shortened the time and distance. It can be done. The Buddha did this with Angulimala. When Angulimala was trying to kill the Buddha, he kept running after him, but the Buddha didn't move, and still he could not catch him. This was because the Buddha used his powers to make the distance always the same."

When the Burmese diplomat U Thant was about to become the new secretary general of the United Nations, Munindra, knowing that U Thant would give an acceptance speech, asked Dipa Ma to go into the future and remember the content. She recited the speech, and Munindra recorded it. A month later, according to Munindra, U Thant gave the exact speech, word for word, just as Dipa Ma had predicted.

Beyond time and space

Dipa Ma said she could go back to the time of the Buddha and listen to his sermons. When I asked her how she did this, she smiled and said, "I went back mind-moment by mind-moment."

I must have looked stunned, because she smiled and said, "Oh, you don't have to do that for Nibbana [enlightenment] to happen." Then she laughed and added, "It was really fun. It just takes a lot of concentration." The look in her eyes when she said this—she looked so free, so pure.

MICHELE MCDONALD

To see with the Divine Eye

❧ Dipa Ma could look inside the body and describe exactly how the brain and heart functioned, with scientific accuracy and at a level that clearly exceeded her own education. She described new devices created in different parts of the world. She would tell Munindra about a new invention, what it looked like, what it was for, where it was kept. Munindra had developed ways of testing his students' abilities, and when he checked up on Dipa Ma's descriptions, he found that they were always 100 percent accurate.

Munindra asked her to see what was going on in the room next to her and describe it to him. He would then verify it. Then he had her systematically extend the power of divine sight to places more and more distant, but places where he could verify the accuracy of her report. She had never been to Bodh Gaya, for instance, and he had her describe it to him—where the Bodhi tree was, what things remained there from antiquity. He had been temple superintendent for many years and knew intimate details of the site.

JACK ENGLER

According to some of her students, Dipa Ma could visit the various realms of existence described in Buddhist cosmology—the heaven and hell realms, for example. She would describe the different beings living there and what was happening all around them. Once in a while, she would offhandedly refer to her travels to other dimensions.

Heaven realm

❀ During the three-month retreat [at Insight Meditation Society], on one of those crystal clear autumn days in New England when the sky is blue with a few puffy clouds and the trees are a display of light and flames and color, we took a walk outdoors. We were sitting by a lake on a rock, and the lake was reflecting all these colors.

There were a number of people there, and one of them said to Dipa Ma, "This must be just like the heaven realms"—we knew she had traveled to the different realms. And she just looked at him and said, "No, it's nothing like it at all. It's okay, but really it doesn't even touch it."

JACK KORNFIELD

Dipa Ma's spiritual powers enabled her to predict her students' futures. "She predicted my teaching career quite elaborately at a time in my life when I wasn't teaching at all," says Joseph Goldstein. "I think she saw the whole course of my life."

Knowledge of the future

❀ Towards the end of my three-month retreat, she looked at me and said, "When you go back

home you will teach metta [lovingkindness medi-
tation] in hospitals." This statement was puzzling
to me since I hadn't had any connection with hospitals. But I thought, "Okay."

I wasn't back home a month before someone
from Children's Hospital called asking if I would
come and run the biofeedback center. It was amazing. So I thought, "Okay, this is the hospital part."
This was a children's hospital, and most of the kids
coming in had stress-related conditions: migraines,
bellyaches, phobias, different things, so I would
teach them metta. I was doing biofeedback as the
context, but I was really teaching them how to do
lovingkindness for themselves and for their critters
and for other kids. I wondered if she sent the job
or just knew it was coming. When I got that phone
call, it was like Dipa Ma was calling me to do that.

MICHELLE LEVEY

Dipa Ma was said to have an uncommonly strong ability
to communicate telepathically with her students.

Beyond language

As my retreat job, I'd been washing dishes
at her house for my last two weeks. When I told
her I was leaving, she offered to do a blessing. She
asked me all kinds of grandmotherly-type questions,
like whether or not I was married and what work
I did. Then she said something in Bengali, put her
hands on my head, and it was like being hit by a
lightning bolt. All of a sudden I felt as if she knew

exactly what was in my mind, and we were having this conversation together that was beyond language. . . . We were communicating on a whole new level, just between the essence of our minds . . . pure communication between her consciousness and mine. I felt like I was hit in the head, in a good way. . . . After the blessing I had this incredible euphoria. I remember walking in the door of the Insight Meditation Society and feeling like I was walking above the ground.

CAROL CONSTANTIAN LAZELL

Mind to mind

Whenever I came to Dipa Ma with some difficulty in my meditation practice, she would look into my eyes with that tranquil, samadhi-like gaze while I was speaking. Before the translator even began, I would feel a tickling in the back of my brain. Something would go "click," and the problem would simply disappear, along with whatever emotional difficulty I might have had with it.

I believe she was capable of psychic or telepathic linking, working directly with others' minds. She taught me silently that the answer to any internal problem was in the basic mind state and not in her words or in any technical adjustment of attention. She gave me the answer to my difficulties by sharing another state of consciousness in which that problem simply didn't exist. It was a sudden, instant shift, like a psychic chiropractic adjustment.

DANIEL BOUTEMY

Enduring smile

❧ I had been studying and training in India for an extended period of time and was going through a lot of difficulty in my life. I was scheduled to return to the States to teach the three-month retreat at IMS. On my way out of the country, I decided to stop in Calcutta and see Dipa Ma. It was, I remember, a terribly hot day: 110 degrees and smoggy and dirty. I paid my respects to her, and we spent a little time talking. As I got up to go, she gave me her usual big bear hug, and then she said a blessing. I got down on my knees, which made me about equal to her in height.

For her extra-special blessing, she would take her hands and stroke your head and your whole body, blow on you, and say Buddhist prayers at the same time. It seemed like a very, very long blessing. At first it just felt kind of nice, but as she kept going it started to feel better and better. By the time she was done, everything felt lit up and open, and I was just grinning from ear to ear.

"Go and teach a good retreat for all of those people," she said. "Go with my blessings." It was like Grandmother sending you off with her good wishes.

I left her place, walked out into the sweltering Calcutta summer, and caught a taxi to Dum Dum Airport. It took about two hours to get there, with the guy leaning on the horn the whole way, dodging between rickshaws and traffic and fumes and pollution and incredible heat and humidity and

poverty and filth. Finally I got to the airport and went through customs, which meant another hour of standing in line with people looking through my stuff and grilling me and stamping my documents. I finally got on my plane and took the two-hour flight to Bangkok.

Bangkok Airport looked like the Los Angeles airport; it was huge. Again, long lines, customs, an hour and a half in a taxi riding through the teeming streets of Bangkok to my hotel. And I did not stop grinning the entire way. The plane ride, long lines, customs, taxi rides, traffic jams, all this—and I'm just sitting there with this big smile on my face. It just would not wear off. It was extraordinary.

JACK KORNFIELD

A rain of blessings

Michelle Levey and her husband, Joel, asked Dipa Ma to do a marriage blessing ceremony with them in 1984.

At the end of the ceremony, she looked at us tenderly and said, "A marriage of meditation will befall you." We knelt down, and Dipa Ma put her hands on our foreheads and gave us a blessing. It felt as if the crowns of our heads were blown off, leaving our heads completely open to all space. Then it was as if she was downloading a transmission directly into our skulls. She poured peace and lovingkindness into our open crowns, and there was a deep, sweet melting and welding of souls together. Neither of us had ever felt any sensation like that before.

After her blessing, we went for a walk in the woods behind the meditation center. It was a clear, crisp December day without a cloud in the sky. Yet, as we were walking through the forest we heard this sound like rice falling on us. It sounded like hail—tcht, tcht, tcht, all over the woods. We were looking up, but the sky was clear and blue. It was like a rain of blessings. We continued to walk, and a strange distortion began happening in time and place. We walked and walked, and we thought we'd end up very far away—but we came out where we started. It was like going for a walk on a mobius strip, thinking we would end up somewhere, yet coming back, turned inside-out or outside-in and put back together in a magical way.

JOEL AND MICHELLE LEVEY

Dipa Ma herself reported an unexpected encounter with the paranormal that came about, she said, because she was following the Buddhist precepts.

The house from nowhere

In Buddhist countries, people observe eight precepts four days a month, and many go to temple on full moon day. One full moon day, a woman friend and I decided to go to the temple.

When we left the house, there was just a little bit of rain, but when we got on the bus, it started to rain heavily. By the time we got off the bus, it was pouring, and the road to the temple was flooded. There were people waiting at the temple for us, but we could go no farther because we were shivering, wet, and quite cold.

Just then a car came by and stopped for us. The gentleman in it said there was a very nice new house nearby. He took us in his car to it. The car stopped at the house, which was fully decorated and had a gate in front of it. We went inside and up the stairs, where we decided to take shelter until the rain stopped. We waited about fifteen minutes, then hurried to the temple.

As soon as we came in, people said, "Oh, you are all wet! How did that happen?" We told them how when we got down from the bus, it was raining heavily and the road was flooded, and that we had found a house and had taken shelter in it. We described the double-story, newly built house to them. But the local people and the monks of the temple, who every day went on alms rounds in the area, said, "We have never seen such a house in the place you describe it."

"Well, of course, there could be some mistake," I told them, "but we did wait there for fifteen to twenty minutes, so there is a house there." There was some discussion back and forth, and finally we said, "All right, let's go and see." We stayed and listened to the dharma talk, and then on our way home went to try and find the house. We went back to the area but could not find it again. How could it be, we wondered, that we had gone inside a house that now was not there? We tried another street, but still we couldn't find anything.

The next day the monk at the temple said he had tried looking for the house where we described it, but he could not find it either. We went back and looked again, still without success. There was a big discussion about this. We finally came to the conclusion that because we were observing sila [moral precepts], practicing the dharma, and had prayed, "May the gods and goddesses protect us from all kinds of harm," they had come to our aid and had made a shelter to get us out of the rain.

This is why I tell you always to try and observe the precepts. Because surely someone will help you and protect you from all kinds of harm. This is from my own experience. There were two of us, so I know it wasn't just a dream or my imagination. The gods and goddesses really came to our aid.

DIPA MA

A student who heard Dipa Ma tell this story remembers the response that followed:

It's true

❀ I liked this small white bundle coming into the hall and telling us stories from her practice to encourage us. One was about a house that appeared miraculously in the rain to shelter her because she was a true servant of the dharma. When we laughed, gently humoring our celebrated teacher, she gazed at us, as uncomprehending of our rational skepticism as we of her faith. "It's true," she said, and we were silent.

LESLEY FOWLER

CHAPTER 10

FEARLESS DAUGHTER OF THE BUDDHA

"I can do anything a man can do."

EVEN AS A widowed single mother, trying to undertake her spiritual path within the confines of a patriarchal and hierarchical Buddhist monastic system, Dipa Ma never doubted that she could reach the highest goal. At that time and place, there was no such thing as a "women's liberation" movement; Dipa Ma simply liberated herself. She once remarked, "I have no fear. I am at peace now."

Before Dipa Ma began meditation practice, she was known to be anxious and dependent on others. Given her personal and cultural background—marriage at age twelve, confinement to her in-laws' house, subordination to her husband—it is astonishing that she became such a free-thinker. She insisted, for example, that her daughter Dipa get a university education and later was supportive when Dipa decided to leave her marriage.

Dipa Ma acknowledged the difficulties of the women around her but insisted that they too could walk the path to liberation. "When you are born in this world," she told her student Pritimoyee Barua, "you have to face many sufferings, especially if you are a woman. A woman's life is very difficult.

But you need not worry about this. You must maintain your practice. You must not worry that you have to take care of your husband and children. If you are in the dharma, everything will happen through it. Everything will be solved through the dharma."

In addition to spiritual counsel, Dipa Ma often gave practical advice to the women who sought her out. "She would lecture me," recalls one Calcutta housewife. "'You should not think that women are helpless. You are not helpless. First of all, you should get an education, and secondly you should do service. If you take care of your economic condition, then you will be independent.'"

Mostly though, Dipa Ma gave strength to others by her own example. She was a master teacher in an almost exclusively male monastic lineage and one of the first female Asian masters to be invited to teach in America. Dipa Ma never made much of those accomplishments, but her powerful example offers inspiration and encouragement to women of every culture.

Challenging tradition

One day, we were all sitting on the floor of Ma's room. It was very crowded and very hot. Munindra was sitting on a chair in the corner talking to Ma's students about the dharma and about their practice. He and I were the only men in the room. While he talked, Ma was sitting on her wooden bed, leaning back against the wall with her eyes closed. It looked like she had dozed off. She hadn't been well, and no one took any notice.

The conversation was about rebirth. Somehow it got on to the rebirths of the Buddha. Obviously

not thinking much about it, since it was part of the tradition, Munindra happened to mention that only men could become Buddhas: to become a Buddha, you had to have taken rebirth in a male body [according to later commentaries, not original texts]. Suddenly, Ma bolted upright, eyes wide open, and said in a tone of spontaneous and utter conviction, "I can do anything a man can do." Our reaction was equally spontaneous: we all laughed, Munindra included. I think we all knew it was absolutely true.

JACK ENGLER

Emotions are not a hindrance

When she mentioned that women could go deeper and more quickly into the practice than men because our minds are softer, that surprised me. That softness brings more emotion, more movement in the mind. A lot of women think that the emotions are a hindrance, but Dipa Ma said, "Women's tendency to be more emotional is not a hindrance to practice." She advised us, "Just watch the emotions and don't identify. Increase the mindfulness of noticing and the concentration."

MICHELLE LEVEY

Gentleness and power

She was a combination of gentleness, no pretense, and power. The fact that she was a woman with so much depth and so much authority was a big deal. Nothing about her was what you would

associate with someone who was going to lead you.
She was not six feet tall and wearing a suit. She
was a skinny, tiny thing. But she was incredibly
thrilling because she did it, she went so far beyond
anything. This meant that I might be able to do it,
too.

KATE WHEELER

A lighthouse

At the time I met her, there were mostly male
role models, male teachers, male Buddhas. To
meet a woman householder who lived with her
daughter and grandson, and who was that enlightened, was more profound than I can ever put into
words. She embodied what I deeply wanted to be
like. Although I was already quite committed to
the practice when I met her, she made freedom seem
attainable. She simply did it. It was not some intellectual idea. For me to be a woman householder,
and to see her as a woman householder, I immediately felt, "If she can do this, I can do it, too."
She is like a lighthouse . . . a light I have oriented
to when I have needed the courage to continue to
walk the path.

MICHELE MCDONALD

Enough

Coming from California, my personal image
of a powerful woman was an amazon who jumps
in the back of a pickup truck with a chainsaw and
is going to sort out the world. But the power of

Dipa Ma was the power of touching the heart. I felt completely known by her. And yet I didn't need to hide or be ashamed, because I felt both totally known and totally loved at the same time.

I remember writing a letter home to my friends after experiencing that kind of love, telling them that if my journey had ended at that point, it would have been good enough. Just having made contact with that profound love was enough.

AJAHN THANASANTI

There's hope for men

❀ Dipa Ma once said, "Women have an advantage over men because they have more supple minds. . . . It may be difficult for men to understand this, because they are men." I asked her, "Is there any hope for us?" She answered, "The Buddha was a man, and Jesus was a man. So there is hope for men, too."

JOSEPH GOLDSTEIN

Research with Dipa Ma and Calcutta housewives

❀ After a year of intensive meditation practice with Munindra, I approached him about beginning my doctoral research on the process and outcomes of insight meditation practice. Part of this was an attempt to validate classic and contemporary accounts of the changes that were reported to take place following enlightenment. Finding subjects was no easy task, because it required identifying practitioners who had experienced at least "First Path," or first stage enlightenment, and gaining their cooperation. To a traditional Indian teacher, this was an extremely unorthodox request, and Munindra was hesitant. After many discussions, he finally agreed to take me to Calcutta and introduce me to some of his most advanced students. Key among these was Dipa Ma, who was initially skeptical. Eventually, however, she introduced me to a number of her students and volunteered herself and her daughter, Dipa, as well. Munindra himself agreed to participate.

For the research, Ma provided all women in middle age or older. It needs to be borne in mind that it is not customary for women to go out alone in India; these women belonged with one exception to the older culture, and most of them were extremely busy with the many responsibilities of running and maintaining a large joint Indian family. The testimony I heard was universal that women make better meditators. I could never quite get to the bottom of this. I asked Ma about it, particularly whether it meant that women tended to go further in the practice than men. I had been told this by several Sayadaws in Burma and by some Indian teachers. Ma simply said she had just as many men who had attained "Path" as women, but that they were not available during the daytime when I would be interviewing and testing.

For more than six months in 1977, Dipa Ma's small room became a research center for the systematic interviewing and psychological testing of

advanced Buddhist practitioners. Most of the interviewing was done during the hot season. If you've
lived through the steamy and suffocating, often sear-
ing heat of a tropical hot season, you can imagine
the conditions in a city like Calcutta, and the effect
of that climate on human and environmental
resources. Electric power was invariably shut off during the hottest hours of the afternoon and evening—
Calcutta's infamous "brown-outs"—to conserve
generator supplies in the city. If we were able to
begin at all—and the heat sometimes made it physically impossible—we often ended in darkness,
soaked through with perspiration. If there was transportation to the old city in the morning, it was often
doubtful whether there would be transportation out
of it again at night. After the monsoon arrived, I'd
sometimes get to her neighborhood and be unable
to get through. The entire street in front of her house
would be flooded up to knee or even thigh level,
and I would have to take a rickshaw the last few
blocks, riding just above the water. Yet somehow
Ma's women students would always be there ahead
of me.

Dipa Ma's test protocols, especially her responses
to the Rorschach, were the most remarkable ever
seen by any of the investigators. The Rorschach test,
which measures not only personality but perception, has been described as reflecting "self-created
reality." In Dipa Ma's case, the Rorschach results
seemed to confirm that she had undergone a profound cognitive-emotional restructuring and psy-

chic integration associated with the deepest levels of enlightenment. Among other things, she spontaneously and effortlessly wove each consecutive response across the entire range of cards into an ongoing narrative that revealed the whole of the teaching of dharma, all without once violating good form perception on each card—a remarkable achievement none of the researchers had ever witnessed [reported in "Mindfulness Meditation: II," in *Transformations of Consciousness*, Ken Wilber, Jack Engler, and Daniel Brown, Boston: Shambhala, 1986].

JACK ENGLER

Mountain of serenity

❧What I remember most about Dipa Ma was the total stillness and unmoving sense of quiet about her. In the winter of 1976–77, my friend Alan Clements and I were spending some time in Calcutta with Munindra and Dipa Ma. One day, Munindra invited us to attend a lecture he was giving that night. We rode over with Munindra and Dipa Ma and arrived very early. Alan, Dipa Ma, and I settled into the front row. Gradually the room began to fill up. Twenty minutes later there were about two hundred people jammed in a room we would not have put more than fifty in. My legs were sort of on top of Dipa Ma's. I was practically on her lap. Then Munindra proceeded to give a five-hour lecture in Bengali. So here we were in a stifling hot, overcrowded room listening for five hours in Bengali! It took everything I had to stay put and I felt as if there were Mexican jumping beans in my body. I was squirming, fidgeting, and sighing. But Dipa Ma was a mountain of serenity. She was in some kind of deep concentration for those five hours. And in my agitation, I kept coming back to her silence and stillness, and it would calm me. That was what got me through. She didn't even seem to notice my struggling; there was no judgment. Just a radiating sense of ease and calm.

CATHERINE INGRAM

Fearless daughters of the Buddha

Dipa Ma and I were on an airplane coming to the States from India. It was very, very turbulent, and at one point the plane hit an air pocket and dropped. Drinks and other objects flew up to the ceiling as the plane dropped downward before hitting stable air again. I kind of screamed. Dipa Ma was sitting across the aisle from me and she reached out and took my hand and she just held it. Then she whispered, "The daughters of the Buddha are fearless."

MARIA MONROE

PART THREE

DIPA MA'S LEGACY

CHAPTER 11

TEN LESSONS
TO LIVE BY

THE STORY OF Dipa Ma's spiritual unfolding is the archetypal tale of all who seek the Way. The stages it describes—setting forth, making a commitment, facing and overcoming difficulties, finding freedom, and sharing one's discoveries with the world—closely parallel those of the Buddha's own journey of transformation.

After his great awakening under the bodhi tree, the Buddha enunciated the Four Noble Truths: first, that suffering exists and is in fact the hallmark of all conditioned existence; second, that its cause is attachment; third, that it is possible to end suffering; and fourth, that there is a path, which he spelled out in detail, that leads away from suffering to the cherished goal of liberation. Buddhist practice, simply put, is about ending suffering, for ourselves and for all beings.

It is this implicit promise—that our own suffering can cease—that first brings many of us to meditation practice. And it is Dipa Ma's life example that can give us the confidence to set forth on this journey. A woman, a mother, a householder, Dipa Ma makes the Buddha's path seem accessible and the great goal of freedom attainable in this very life.

What follows are some of the lessons we can derive from Dipa Ma's essential teachings. May they be of help to you in your own journey of liberation.

LESSON ONE
Choose one meditation practice and stick with it

"If you want to progress in meditation, stay with one technique."

For those beginning the spiritual journey, Dipa Ma was adamant about commitment to one style of meditation. Don't give up, and don't jump around from practice to practice. Find a technique that suits you, and keep going until you find your "edge," the point where difficulties start to arise.

A common mistake many Western spiritual seekers make is to interpret difficulties as a problem with a particular practice. Then, when the going gets tough, the tough go "spiritual shopping." From the vantage point of that uncomfortable edge, some other practice always looks better. "Maybe I should do Tibetan chanting . . . or Sufi dancing." In fact, difficulties usually are a reliable sign that the practice is working.

Take Dipa Ma's advice to heart. Stick with the practice you've chosen through difficulty and doubt, through inspiration and stagnation, through the inevitable ups and downs. If you can stay committed to your practice through the darkest of times, wisdom will dawn.

LESSON TWO
Meditate every day

"Practice now. Don't think you will do more later."

Dipa Ma stated firmly that if you want peace, you must practice regularly. She insisted that students find time for formal meditation practice every day, even if only for five minutes. If that proved impossible, she advised, "At least when you are in bed at night, notice just one in-breath and one out-breath before you fall asleep."

Besides formal sitting on the cushion, Dipa Ma urged students to make every moment of their lives a meditation. Many of them were busy people who found it difficult to set aside any time at all. Dipak Chowdhury told Dipa Ma that it was impossible for him to practice because he had a very full schedule at the bank where he worked. He explained that he spent his workdays doing calculations, and that his job required him to be continually on the move, too busy and too restless even to think about meditation. Dipa Ma wouldn't hear of this; she insisted that meditation is always possible, that it is not separate from life. "If you are busy, then busyness is the meditation," she told him. "When you do calculations, know that you are doing calculations. Meditation is to know what you are doing. If you are rushing to the office, then you should be mindful of 'rushing.' When you are eating, putting on your shoes, your socks, your clothes, you must be mindful. It is all meditation! Even when you are cutting your nails, put your mind there. Know that you are cutting your nails."

For Dipa Ma, mindfulness wasn't something she did, it was who she was—all the time. The best attitude with which to approach this practice, she said, is with trust and willingness. When your mind wanders, simply begin again. Dipa Ma made it clear that there is nothing wrong with lapses of mindfulness. "It happens to everyone. It is not a permanent problem. Don't worry, just start again. Always maintain your effort, patience, and faith." Even when you lose energy and motivation, she advised, just notice that, then shift to another mindfulness practice—walking, awareness in ordinary activity, or sitting—in which more motivation is present.

LESSON THREE
Any situation is workable

"Each of us has enormous power. It can be used to help ourselves and help others."

The Buddha left his wife and child in order to pursue his awakening. But Dipa Ma, out of necessity, found her path to freedom within the context of motherhood and ordinary household life. Her message to women (and men) everywhere is that you don't have to leave your family to reach high states of spiritual understanding. You can be a spouse and parent and still pursue the dharma.

Even though initially she thought that she would have to give up her daughter to go to a monastery and practice in solitude, Dipa Ma came to understand that she could make her family part of the journey. Dipa Ma's approach was a radical inclusiveness—everything and the kitchen sink.

"There is nothing ultimately to cling to in this world," Dipa Ma taught, "but we can make good use of everything in it. Life is not to be rejected. It is here. And as long as it is here and we are here, we can make the best use of it."

Dipa Ma wasn't attached to a particular teacher, place, or lifestyle. The whole world was her monastery. Sharon Kreider remembers, "At my idealistic age of twenty—when I wanted to believe if I sat long enough with the right teacher, everything would be okay—she showed me it was about being awake to much more. She was an example of how to be a true mother to the world. To be a true mother is to feel life intensely. To be a true mother is to embrace whatever comes along, with awareness, and to make all circumstances my teachers."

LESSON FOUR
Practice patience

"Patience is one of the most important virtues for developing mindfulness and concentration."

Patience is forged by constantly meeting the edge. If you stay with your meditation practice, it is inevitable that difficulties will arise. In the most challenging situations, merely showing up, being present, may be all that is possible—and it may be enough.

Kate Wheeler recounts the effects of this kind of patience in Dipa Ma's life: "She had seen her mind go through every kind of suffering and was able to sit through it. Later, when she came out of that fire, there was something very determined, almost frightening about how she could look at you, because she had seen herself. There was nowhere to hide. She exemplified that you can't just sit around thinking about getting enlightened. You have to take hold of these truths at the deepest level of your heart."

Dipa Ma's daughter talks about her mother's patience. "The day before she died, Rishi, who was eleven at the time, was misbehaving when I was getting ready for work. I got very angry. I was trying to hit him, and he hid behind my mother. She wouldn't let me touch him. I was very upset and cried to her, 'You don't know how mad he has made me. I want to punish him!' My mother came to me with a mild, slow voice and said, 'Dipa, you are my daughter, and you too were silly once. I did not throw you out of the house for being silly.' She talked about being affectionate and patient and talking slowly. It was a teaching I remember."

Patience is a lifetime practice, to be developed and refined over time. According to Dipa Ma, patience is essential in maturing the mind and therefore is one of the most important qualities to cultivate.

LESSON FIVE
Free your mind

"Your mind is all stories."

Dipa Ma did not say that the mind is mostly stories; she said that there is *nothing* in the mind but stories. These are the personal dramas that create and maintain the sense of individual identity: who we are, what we do, what we are and are not capable of. Without our being aware of it, the endless series of such thoughts drives and limits our lives. And yet those stories are without substance.

Dipa Ma challenged students' beliefs in their stories, their attachment to the stories. When someone said, "I can't do that," she would ask, "Are you sure?" or "Who says?" or "Why not?" She encouraged students to observe the stories, to see their emptiness, and to go beyond the limitations they impose. "Let go of thinking," she urged. "Meditation is not about thinking."

At the same time, Dipa Ma taught that the mind is not an enemy to be gotten rid of. Rather, in the process of befriending the mind, in getting to know and accept it, it ceases to be a problem. Dipa Ma knew the freedom that follows that process: she lived in a state of thought-free awareness.

In a group interview, Jack Kornfield innocently asked, "What is it like in your mind?"

Dipa Ma smiled, closed her eyes, and quietly answered, "In my mind there are three things: concentration, lovingkindness, and peace."

Jack, not sure if he had heard correctly, asked, "Is that all?"

"Yes, that is all," Dipa Ma replied.

The room was silent. Then there were a few sighs and quiet laughs, followed by Jack's barely audible whisper, "How wonderful."

LESSON SIX
Cool the fire of emotions

"Anger is a fire."

When someone came to visit Dipa Ma, it didn't matter who it was, or what emotional state they were embroiled in, or what the circumstances were, Dipa Ma treated each person with complete, compassionate acceptance.

Can we offer the same acceptance to the emotions that arise in us? Can we see our emotional states as visitors to be treated with kindness? Can we simply allow anger and other emotions to arise and pass away, without reacting in ways that might be harmful?

"A lot of incidents happen in daily life which are undesirable," Dipa Ma said. "Sometimes I experience some irritation, but my mind remains cool. Irritation comes and passes. My mind isn't disturbed by this. Anger is a fire. But I don't feel any heat. It comes and it dies right out."

Dipa Ma's example is inspiring, but aren't there certain occasions when anger might be appropriate? Aren't there at least some situations when it's justified? For Dipa Ma the answer was simple: no, anger is never justified. And she found ways to navigate through life without it.

Sylvia Boorstein, who hosted Dipa Ma in her California home in 1980, said that her husband once challenged Dipa Ma on this point. "Dipa Ma was talking about the importance of maintaining tranquillity and equanimity and non-anger, and my husband asked her, 'Could you do that? What if someone were in some way to jeopardize your grandson Rishi, to threaten him?'"

"I would stop him, of course," Dipa Ma replied, "but without anger."

LESSON SEVEN
Have fun along the way

"I am quite happy. If you come to meditate, you will also be happy."

Jack Engler asked Dipa Ma about the place of fun in Buddhist practice. "This all sounds very gray," he said. "Getting rid of the passion, getting rid of anger, getting rid of desire. It seems like a kind of gray existence. Where's the juice?"

"Oh, you don't understand!" Dipa Ma burst out laughing. "There is so much sameness in ordinary life. We are always experiencing everything through the same set of lenses. Once greed, hatred, and delusion are gone, you see everything fresh and new all the time. Every moment is new. Life was dull before. Now, every day, every moment is full of taste and zest."

Eric Kolvig remembers a group interview in which Dipa Ma's playfulness was expressed in an unforgettable image. "Dipa Ma's grandson became upset about something in the kitchen. He let the world know about it in the willful way that is common in two-year-olds and dictators. She called him to the couch, where she laid him face down across her lap and comforted him by stroking his back and patting his tush—an age-appropriate blessing. A blue and yellow plastic toy dump truck lay beside them. With the profound serenity that never left her, Dipa Ma picked up the toy, placed it upside down on her head, and continued with the dharma point she was making. She kept it on for the rest of the interview. That is how I will always remember her:

patting the butt of the pacified child
on her lap and discoursing on the
dharma with a blue and yellow dump
truck on her head. Dipa Ma was a
great spiritual warrior, the greatest I

have known. On her head that toy truck became the warrior's
noble helmet. I say that only half in jest."

LESSON EIGHT
Simplify

"Live simply. A very simple life is good for everything. Too much luxury is a hindrance to practice."

Even though Dipa Ma and her family lived in two tiny
rooms, most visitors perceived those rooms as spacious and
filled with light. One student observed that while we in the
West think we need a lot of physical space, what Dipa Ma had
was a vast psychic space.

In every way, Dipa Ma lived in the greatest simplicity. She
refrained from socializing. She did not engage in unnecessary
talk. She didn't involve herself in other people's concerns, especially complaints. Her guideline for herself and her students
was to live honestly and never blame others.

Often Dipa Ma simply rested in silence. "Whenever I get
time alone, I always turn my mind inward," she said. She did
not spend time at any activity that was unnecessary to her life.

Just as in meditation we practice giving our full attention
to one thing at a time, Dipa Ma did each thing completely
without worrying about the next. "Thoughts of the past and
future," she said, "spoil your time." In whatever she did, she
was fully present, with ease, stillness, and simplicity.

Dipa Ma encouraged her American students to simplify their material needs. In entering one household she exclaimed, "Why so many things? Why so many pairs of shoes? Why ten boxes of tea? Why? The accumulation of things only increases the want. You will not find any pleasure in plenty."

LESSON NINE
Cultivate the spirit of blessing

"If you bless those around you, this will inspire you to be attentive in every moment."

Dipa Ma made of her life one continuous blessing. She offered blessings to all. She blessed people from head to toe, blowing on them, chanting over them, stroking their hair.

Dipa Ma invited a student who was an airline pilot to send lovingkindness and blessings to his passengers and his colleagues while he was flying the plane. She said it would make him more alert and make everyone happy as well.

Her blessings were not reserved exclusively for people. Before boarding an airplane she would bestow a blessing upon it. Riding in a car was an opportunity to offer a blessing not only to the vehicle but also to the driver and to the men who pumped the gas.

In one of her very first teachings in America, Dipa Ma said, "Meditation is love." Her spirit of blessing throughout the day was a living example of this teaching. She reminds us that true meditation is about how we care for ourselves and the world; and that ultimately, meditation is the continual movement of love which, similar to one of Dipa Ma's blessings, encompasses nothing less than everyone and everything.

LESSON TEN
It's a circular journey

"Meditation integrates the whole person."

Buddhists speak metaphorically of "leaving the world" and "coming back to the world," but in truth there is neither leaving the world nor returning to it. We can't leave or return to our essence, to the rock-bottom truth of our being, because it is and has always been right here, hidden only by a thin film of ignorance. You don't discover it; rather you allow it to come forth, to emerge from the cloud of unknowing that surrounds you. Seeing into your true nature means realizing that you are inextricably bound to everyone and everything that lives, that you are, indeed, responsible for all that takes place in the world.

The beauty of the spiritual journey is that the path invariably takes us back around to our point of departure. When Dipa Ma suffered her childlessness, her husband wisely suggested that she adopt everyone as her own child. But in those difficult days before she encountered the teachings that would transform her life, she was lost in sadness for what she lacked, trying to "fill a hole." By the end of her life, though, Dipa Ma had indeed become a mother to all. In place of that hole that needed to be filled, there simply was a heart open to all.

CHAPTER 12

IN THE PRESENCE
OF A MASTER:
QUESTIONS AND ANSWERS

THE FOLLOWING QUESTIONS and answers were recorded in interviews with Dipa Ma in India in the 1970s and at Insight Meditation Society in the 1980s.

How do I practice vipassana [insight] meditation?

Sit [with your back straight]. Close your eyes and follow the rising and falling, the rising and falling of the abdomen as you breathe. Feel the breath. When watching the breathing in and out, ask yourself, "Where is the touch of the breath?" Keep your mind on the touch only. You are to do nothing with the breathing, only feel the touch. If it is heavy, let it be heavy. It if is short, let it be short. If it is fine, let it be fine. Just feel it.

When your mind wanders away, notice this and say to yourself, "Thinking," and then come back again to the rising and falling of the breath. If you feel a sensation somewhere else, like pain in the leg, then take your mind to the pain and note, "Pain." And when it goes away or fades, then again come to watching the touch of the breath. If restlessness comes, note "restlessness."

If you hear a noise, say to yourself, "Hearing, hearing," then again come back to the feeling of the breath. If memories come, know them as "memories." Anything you see, anything that comes to mind, just be aware of it. If you see visions or lights, just note "seeing" or "lights." There is no need to keep any of it, to make it stay. Simply observe.

In insight meditation, you are observing the rising and falling of the breath and the phenomena that arise in the mind and body. So there is a shifting of the mind from sensations felt, both painful and pleasurable, to thoughts as well. Whatever is happening is to be noticed, then that will go away, and another thing will come. In this way, insight practice is a method of observation. All six senses [the mind being the sixth] will arise. Just watch them arise and pass away and come back to the feeling of the breath. Anything you see, anything that comes to mind, just be aware of it.

What is the purpose of insight meditation?

The purpose of insight meditation is to eliminate the Ten Fetters, which are the knots or obstructions in your mind. Very slowly, by observing every moment with awareness, you come to open these knots. The Ten Fetters are self-illusion [that is, the illusion of a separate self], doubt, attachment to rites and rituals, lust, ill-will, craving, craving for fine material existence, conceit, restlessness, ignorance.

At each stage of enlightenment, slowly, one by one, some of the fetters are extinguished, until the fourth stage, or arahantship, when all the fetters are gone. The fetters are related to birth in the same way that oil feeds the light of a lamp. The fetters are like oil in your mind. As the oil becomes less and less, the light from the wick becomes less and less. Finally, when the oil is gone, the light is gone. Once they are extinguished, the cycle of rebirth ends. From this, you can understand that birth and rebirth are in your hands.

What should I do if I fall asleep during my sitting practice?

There is no harm in this. Yogis sometimes sleep in this way. It is called "yogi sleep." This happens. Don't worry about it. When I first started doing meditation I was always crying because I wanted to follow the instructions with full vigor and enthusiasm, but I could not, due to sleepiness. I could not even do standing and walking meditation properly due to sleepiness. For five years prior to this time I had tried to sleep, but could not. And now here I was, trying to do meditation, and sleepiness was keeping me from it. I was using my full energy to drive away the sleepiness, but still I could not do it. Then one day, all of a sudden, I came to such a state that my sleepiness disappeared, and no sleep came to me even if I sat for some hours.

Is karma like an accounting record that is stored? If so, where is it stored?

Everybody has the wheel of karma. It is in your own hands; nobody can store it. As you act, it is stored. It flows on with the stream of consciousness. The day you take birth, this karma comes with you. Others can only show you the way; they cannot change your karma. No one can willfully take on the karma of another. You have to do the work. Because of karma, some people progress quickly, and some progress slowly in meditation. Some have a lot of pain, and some don't.

If there is no soul, then who sees, hears, and knows?

Wisdom.

What should one do when energy and effort are low?

Sometimes the energy will be low. Sometimes the energy will be high. Sometimes the effort will be low. Sometimes the effort will be high. But you are to note only "low energy, low effort." If you notice it when it is low, automatically it will be corrected. Know "low energy" or "high energy" until a sort of medium energy, medium effort is there. It should be done quietly, slowly, and with ease. Energy and effort are regulated by noticing them. One should not be a victim of energies.

How can you love and not attach at the same time?

A simple example is that of water. Nonattachment means you flow on top of the water. You don't plunge into it. You stay afloat without going under.

Is it true that a meditator needs a vegetarian diet?

The question of vegetarian or non-vegetarian does not matter. What matters is the mentality. Even if you take a vegetarian diet, with a mind polluted with greed or hatred or delusion, your vegetarian diet will become a non-vegetarian diet. This is what the Buddha taught. If your mind is free from greed and hatred, your non-vegetarian diet will become a vegetarian diet for you. For any action—physical, verbal, or mental—the Buddha gave the importance to intention.

Sometimes I feel suicidal and depressed.

Depression and suicidal feelings are a disease. It happens sometimes even to a highly developed meditator. Try to develop a practical outlook. On the one hand, you must know the result of committing suicide: it is an act from which you cannot rescue yourself for many successive rebirths. Also try to remember that human life is most precious. Don't waste it. Better to engage yourself in vipassana and be happy.

Is intelligence important to progress in meditation?

No. I have no intellect at all. And I didn't know anything about meditation or states of consciousness. I had a simple faith in the dharma. I felt there was something there for me. With this simple faith, I began.

What is the use of mindfulness?

Let me tell you an example. If I told you there was some jewelry hidden somewhere and I asked you to go and collect it, you would leave your house and go to where it was hidden. On the way to find the jewelry, you might see a fight break out, and you would stop and watch. But after a while, you would proceed. You might see a marriage party going by with their drums, and you would stand there, but again, after a while you would proceed. You might see a street rally, and you would stop and later proceed. If you are not mindful, you cannot reach your destination to collect the jewelry I have asked you to get. But whenever there is mindfulness, even if there are interruptions and obstacles you will not get lost, you will proceed on. Mindfulness allows you to reach your goal. It is the "great vocation" in life which leads to the end of suffering.

Did most of the important changes in your life come about during times of intensive practice or as you lived your daily life in a meditative way?

The great changes happened during intensive training. And then I cultivated them in my daily life. They became deeper and deeper that way.

Did your sorrow and lamentation slowly drop away, or did it happen quickly as the result of an insight?

Gradually I could feel it was going away. And then after more meditation practice I acquired some wisdom, and the whole thing disappeared.

Who should teach meditation?

There are two things for teaching. One is knowledge and understanding. The other is attainment, first or second stage of enlightenment. [The following is Jack Kornfield's paraphrase of the rest of Dipa Ma's answer.] The paramis [perfected virtues] for being a teacher are different from the paramis for practice. Basically they are different skills. Some people may have quite good potential in their meditation and their spiritual life, and others might have a fine ability to communicate and teach. The two aren't necessarily the same. But for someone to teach, they would hopefully have both qualities of good and deep experience in their spiritual life and the capacity to communicate it to others.

What is the best thing to do when sense desires are strong?

Meditate and focus your attention on them directly. Know that they are strong. Get to know them. . . . Through knowing sense desire when it occurs, you can overcome it. You can stay in the world of sense desires and still be a good Buddhist, because you can be "out of the world" at the same time, in the sense of not being drawn in or attached.

Has your basic understanding of life changed?

My outlook has changed greatly. Before, I was too attached to everything. I was possessive. I wanted things. But now it feels like I'm floating, detached. I am here, but I don't want things, I don't want to possess anything. I'm living, that's all. That's enough.

How do I practice metta [lovingkindness] meditation?

[The following is a combination of Dipa Ma's tape-recorded instructions and recollections from Michelle Levey, who for more than twenty years has practiced the lovingkindness meditation she learned from Dipa Ma. You may choose to devote an entire meditation session to lovingkindness practice, or you may decide to begin or end with it. Eventually, the five distinct stages may be combined in one session, but at the beginning, it is best to focus on one at a time.]

First stage

The first stage is to love yourself, to be a best friend to yourself. Begin by extending lovingkindness to yourself. You can use the following words and mental images to guide you in generating and directing your feelings of lovingkindness.

Let me be free of enemies.
Let me be free of dangers.
Let me be free of mental anxieties.
Let me pass my time with good body and happy mind.

"Enemies" means both outward enemies and also being an enemy to yourself. Enemies can exist in the realm of our feelings, from the slightest irritation to the full force of hatred and ill will toward self or others.

While saying these phrases silently, hold an image of yourself steadily and clearly. If you can't visualize yourself, try to remember how you look in the mirror. If this is difficult, try actually looking in a mirror or at a recent photo of yourself until you can see yourself clearly in your mind's eye.

Repeat the phrases in order. If your mind wanders and you forget what phrase you're on, start from the beginning, "Let me be free of enemies." Bringing the mind back to the phrases again and again will deepen your concentration.

It is important to drop into the meaning and feeling beneath the words, letting the words be your guide, keeping you on track and anchored in the practice. Hold the feeling of well-being for yourself in your heart and mind, along with the mental image, and continue to repeat the phrases silently to yourself for as much time as your session permits.

When it is done deeply, when you feel that you truly love yourself, when you can hold the image of yourself clearly and steadily, then if you wish, you may go on to the next stage, which is to extend loving-kindness to a good friend.

Second stage

Using the same phrases as before, direct the loving-kindness to a good friend or teacher who has been kind to you. As you did while sending lovingkindness to yourself, now hold the image of this friend clearly and steadily in your mind, and extend lovingkindness towards him or her.

May you be free of enemies.

May you be free of dangers.
May you be free of mental anxieties.
May you pass your time with good body and happy mind.

When you find that you love your friend as yourself,
or when you find that you can hold the image of the
friend clearly and steadily along with the phrases, then
if you wish, you may go on to the next stage.

Third stage

The next category of beings to send lovingkindness to
are called "the sufferers"—any beings or groups of beings
who are suffering. Whereas before you held a stable,
one-pointed image of one person, now begin to expand
your focus to encompass a larger number of beings.
Begin by holding in mind one whole group of beings
who are suffering. Extend your lovingkindness to these
beings the same way you did before with yourself and
your friend.

May you be free of enemies.
May you be free of dangers.
May you be free of mental anxieties.
May you pass your time with good body and happy mind.

If spontaneous images arise of other groups of suffering people, such as people in hospitals or in wars,
then it's fine to direct your lovingkindness to them, meditating in a dynamic way with the flow of changing
images. Continue reciting the phrases while gradually
focusing more and more on the feelings of lovingkindness behind the words.

From the foundation of truly and deeply loving
yourself, see how self-love is the foundation and the

fuel for loving others. In loving yourself, you love your friend as yourself. Then you love the sufferers like your friend, which is like yourself. With continued practice, all groups will merge into one.

Fourth stage

In the fourth stage, lovingkindness and equanimity blend together. The practice is to hold a vast sense of all living beings in one's mind and to send metta to them all equally—friends, people who suffer, people for whom your feelings are neutral, those with whom you have difficulty, all beings everywhere.

May all beings be free of enemies.
May all beings be free of dangers.
May all beings be free of mental anxieties.
May all beings pass their time with good body and happy mind.

To do this, allow your mind to become lovingkindness. Do this by attending primarily to the feeling of lovingkindness: the words and phrases you've used up to this point have simply been pointers to the feeling. Allow your mind to become lovingkindness, and rest in that with equanimity, not favoring where it goes.

Fifth stage

The crowning stage of metta meditation is to combine all the stages and focus for a while on each of the stages in one meditation session. Practiced in this way, the meditation becomes like a symphony of lovingkindness in which you start with yourself, and open, open, open, until you finally come to rest in equanimity.

THE LEGACY CONTINUES

THE TEACHING OF a great spiritual master can take many forms. One of the most powerful and mysterious is the teaching that comes from pure presence. As many people attest, it was Dipa Ma's simple, clear, compassionate way of being in the world that offered the most compelling encouragement to walk the path of dharma.

Even after Dipa Ma's death, numerous students continue to experience her presence. Dipa Ma also has appeared to people who have never met her, and reports of her presence continue decades after her death. For many students, seeing Dipa Ma in a vision or dream or sensing her presence as energy is followed by a period of deep concentration and peace. One meditation teacher who regularly experiences Dipa Ma's presence says, "You could call it grace. Whatever it is, when it happens, I am grateful."

She is still teaching me

I was living at a retreat center in the Southwest, writing this book. On the wall above my desk I had taped a three-by-five color photocopy of Dipa Ma in meditation. One day, after hanging up a new and better photo, I tossed the photocopy in the trash. Then I felt a pang: "Maybe I shouldn't throw this photo away." I vaguely remembered some Buddhist admonition about throwing dharma things away being disrespectful, bringing bad karma.

For a moment I wondered, "Will this action come back to haunt me?"

"Nonsense," I finally decided, "it's only a photocopy. It's already in the trash and going to the dump. I'm putting up a better photo. I'm not being disrespectful."

End of debate.

Months later, one hot summer afternoon, I was helping dismantle our ramshackle outdoor porch. When we pulled the sheetrock off the wall, at the far end of the framing I saw a desert packrat nest. Mother packrats collect an amazing array of colorful objects, and it's always interesting to see what shows up in their nests.

As I moved closer, something caught my eye. In the middle of the nest, perfectly intact and cradled in pieces of cactus, tin foil, bits of red plastic, rat feces, and a blue ballpoint pen, was the photo of Dipa Ma in meditation. Beaming at me.

As it happens, that was the very same photograph I had spotted in room M101 on my first visit to the Insight Meditation Society so many years before. My very first encounter with Ma. A beginning, and an ending—all one.

She is still teaching me.

AMY SCHMIDT

In the midst of suffering, a being of light

❧ When I am in a lot of suffering, when I have clients who are in horrible pain, or when I am in a circumstance where there is much suffering, Dipa Ma "appears." Not in the sense of her actually being here, but more a quality of her presence in the midst of the suffering. She appears in my thinking in those circumstances.

When this happens, my balance becomes better, and there is an increase in compassion. She has appeared on a number of occasions when I was doing body-work with someone in acute pain. She is a reminder to me that "In the worst of suffering, there is still a being of light."

ROY BONNEY

The strength of my practice is with you

❀ I feel very much as if I've continued to receive her teachings. One example occurred right after she died, in early September 1989.

I sat the three-month course at IMS that year, and I was having one particularly physically painful sitting, and a vow came up within me of, "I will sit through this pain, I have the strength to look at this." When it got quite excruciating, I suddenly felt very full of Dipa Ma. I felt her presence and her offering: "The strength of my practice is here with you." There was all this, and then a burst of energy, and I was able to move through the pain.

JANNE STARK

Humility

❀ Around the time of my monastic ordination, even though it was several years after Dipa Ma had

died, it felt as if she came to speak to me, saying
that my job was to learn about humility. Looking
back over my years of monastic life, I realize how
profoundly true this has been.

We planted two trees in memory of Dipa Ma.
The first was in the nun's garden at Cittaviveka
[Chithurst] Buddhist Monastery in England. The
abbot and some other monks joined a few of us
nuns down at the nuns' cottage where we found
a spot and dug a hole.

At the bottom of the hole was a piece of pottery. When we took the pottery out, we saw that
on it was written the Lord's Prayer. It felt like a powerful sign that transcended religions.

Some years later, the memorial to Dipa Ma was
expanded to include a bridge across the stream in
the nuns' garden. I was particularly pleased with
the idea because the image of crossing the stream
has a deep association with her in my heart.

However, in the details of negotiating con-
struction of the bridge, something happened that
made me angry. In fact, I was absolutely livid, utterly
furious. Later, I went down to the tree we'd planted
and saw that the tree had become sick.

Eventually the tree died. It was a clear message
to me about the effects of anger. A memorial for
Dipa Ma could not be made with unresolved anger.
Eventually the bridge was completed with its
memorial plaque honoring Dipa Ma.

We also planted an oak tree for Dipa Ma in the

orchard at Amaravati Buddhist Monastery in Hert-fordshire, England, in the Buddha Grove. This tree has continued to grow and is strong and healthy.

Often when I felt upset or challenged, I would walk to the tree and sit and chant a mantra and sing to Dipa Ma. Sometimes I set up an altar in the tree and would do walking meditation. When I did this, usually after some time I would feel my whole body relax into the peaceful feeling of Dipa Ma's love and understanding, and although the external situation hadn't shifted, the problem was no longer so pressing.

AJAHN THANASANTI

Ever present

She is like a steady, unflickering candlelight of the dharma that has just stayed in my heart. She is ever present for me.

When she was alive and even now that she's dead, her presence is not very far away. When I meditate, the greatest gift is being able to find her on the inside. She told me, "You will know the answers for yourself from inside. Keep listening."

MICHELLE LEVEY

Her guidance never wavers

I went with her to the airport when she was leaving IMS in 1980. I had spent a lot of time with her, and I was feeling intense grief. I was crying, my heart was heavy, and the pain was incredibly strong, just like when my mother left when I was three and a half. Ma turned to me and looked into my eyes.

"Don't worry," she said. "I'll always be with you."

She took her hands and put them on my heart, and in that instant, the pain, the grief, everything disintegrated, and I was filled with light. I kept this experience to myself for years and years and years and never shared it with anybody because it was so profound and hard to express.

For the longest time I was skeptical about her "I will always be with you," but her presence has stayed with me and has strengthened. I started practicing mindfulness two decades ago, and Dipa Ma's guidance has never wavered.

Other people can feel these moments as well. A few years ago I went to a purifying ceremony with a Lakota Sioux elder who was taught by her ancestors. At one point in the ceremony I was completely terrified. I felt a death, a death of self. I was not sure I could go through with it. I kept wanting to leave the ceremony because I believed it was too intense for me to finish. With tears streaming down my face, I put my cheek to the earth and closed my eyes and just thought of Dipa Ma.

In that instant I was flooded with light, and the fear vanished. A deep peace filled my being, all from bringing Dipa Ma to mind. At one point the Lakota ceremony elder looked at me and said, "You're filled with light."

Intuitively I know she hasn't come back into

bodily form. She is enjoying where she is teaching now. Sometimes I get a strong, vivid picture of where she is. There is a lot of light. Her presence is felt by a flooding of light.

She is still guiding us on this earthly plane for however long we need her. She is one of our guardians. She watches over us.

SHARON KREIDER

If I can do it, you can do it

❧ On the three-month retreat, I was having lots of difficulty. All I was doing was struggle, struggle, struggle for quite a long time.

During one meditation period, I found myself wishing I had known Dipa Ma and wondering, "Could she still be in touch somehow?"

Suddenly I had a sense of her being present and in communication with me. I felt her strong encouragement and the words, "If I can do it, you can do it. "

After this experience, I went into a very concentrated state that lasted for a couple of weeks.

ANONYMOUS

To love the unlovable

❧ I had never heard of Dipa Ma until a friend began telling me what a great teacher she had been and suggested that I find out more about her. A few days later, as I was sitting alone in my apartment reading an account of her life, I suddenly began to feel a profound peace; it was overwhelming and beautiful and unlike anything I had ever experienced. Every fear and anxiety just disappeared and I felt at ease with everything in my life; total peace and a complete opening. As this was happening, I sensed a physical presence in front of me and slightly to the right. The sensation of someone standing near lasted about five minutes.

For two days afterward, I felt as if I were floating and the things that usually caused me anxiety and worry lost their importance; there just wasn't a need to connect with them as usual. It was as though I had stepped through a doorway into a different way of being. I had never really understood what my teachers meant when they talked about "the heart opening," but within that experience, I began to see that the heart only unfolds when there is no fear.

Ever since that day, a phrase keeps running through my mind and I think it's from Dipa Ma. The words are: "Love the unlovable."

PAMELA KIRBY

Who is this person?

When I was on a metta retreat at Insight Meditation Society, one night Joseph Goldstein gave a wonderful talk about compassion in which he told stories about his teacher Dipa Ma. After the talk, I left the meditation hall and felt pulled by a strong energy source. It was as if my body was a compass, and it was being moved in a direction towards something. It was clearly an external force and not something internal or emotional.

After some initial hesitation, I decided to explore the energy—where it was coming from, where it was leading to. After several turns and explorations, I realized it was pulling me upstairs in the building, and down the hall to room M101. As I had my hand on the doorknob to the room, I knew that whatever was behind the door was the source of this energy.

Once in the room, the intensity of the energy was almost overwhelming. My body was shaking, and I sat down in one corner.

Then, in the direction from which the energy was emanating, I noticed a picture of what I thought was a man in white sitting on a lawn.

It was as if a vortex of energy was pulling me toward the photo. I went over and picked up the photo, and sure enough the energy changed if I moved the photo away from me, from side to side or up and down.

I wondered, "Who is this person?" And then I felt, "I'm going to have to pack up my family and go move to be with this teacher. This is too powerful to ignore."

I stayed in the room for sometime after and meditated with the picture, bathing in this intense feeling. This experience created a feeling of concentration, love, and peace that lasted for days, and in fact is still affecting me on a deeper level.

Later I found out from a staff member that the photo was not of a man, but of Dipa Ma.

DAVID GRANT

In the lap of compassion

❁ One night I had a dream about Dipa Ma. In the dream I was alone in a room with her, sobbing and sobbing. No words, no thoughts, just touching the deepest pain. My head was lying in her lap. She was gently patting me on the back as she tenderly rocked me back and forth.

The next day I told Sharon Salzberg about the dream. I told her how much I wished I could have met Dipa Ma. Sharon turned to me with a smile and said, "You just did."

MYOSHIN KELLEY

Put your head at their feet

❁ After Dipa Ma died, I was having quite a lot of difficulty with someone in my life. Dipa Ma came to me in a dream, and in her fierce and uncompromising way, she told me to bow down to this person and to put my forehead at their feet. She also told me to send lovingkindness as I bowed. Just the thought of doing this changed my relationship with this person. It was so humbling. I think of this image often when I'm really stuck with anyone—touching my head to their feet with Dipa Ma's encouragement. After I bow down, I've also learned that it's important to stand up and express the truth and take action when necessary.

MICHELE MCDONALD

Without the story

❁ One afternoon Dipa Ma's presence unexpectedly came to teach me. I had recently suffered a business failure, causing a large financial loss. On one particular day following the loss, I had the flu and was trying to rest, when a truck full of my defunct inventory arrived unannounced and the driver proceeded to unload forty boxes onto my front lawn. Sitting in the grass with these piles of boxes, queasy, and broke, I felt quite a good dose of despair and self-pity. With my head in my hands, quietly from within, I heard something. It was a soft laughter which gradually got louder and louder. Suddenly I saw Dipa Ma's face and she was laughing and laughing. In between her peels of laughter she chided, "This project was about dana (generosity). It was never about making money or breaking even. This was a story you made up! What would it be like without this story?" My answer was a smile, and the realization that I was in fact someone sitting on a front lawn, surrounded by boxes, on a summer afternoon, with no problem at all.

AMY SCHMIDT

Evoking Dipa Ma's presence

Some practitioners offer ideas on how to evoke the power of her presence.

❁ I pray to her all the time. She is part of me in so many ways. Her presence is never not there. One thing that's missing in vipassana is the whole devotional aspect, so I've been reintroducing this into my daily practice.

I start every morning by calling to mind all the Buddhas and Bodhisattvas, the masters, all the enlightened beings. I feel their presence, pray to them, ask for guidance and for them to be an example to me. Then, throughout the day, I bring these realized beings to mind. Ma is one of them.

JACK ENGLER

The Tibetans sometimes talk about how the energy of Milerapa's practice is still here. I feel that Dipa Ma's commitment, her passion, her determination, how much she cut through, how much she went beyond—that's a force that is still available. By remembering her, by thinking about her, it makes that power available. We can call upon the power of her enlightenment.

When difficulties come, I try to imagine, "Where is Dipa Ma?" or connect with that visceral sense of her—her ironlike quality that I can still feel. When I remember her feeling or image, then I stop being so immersed in the stories my mind is telling me. I remember that it is possible to be past this.

KATE WHEELER

Over many years, I have had quite a few teachers. Often at the beginning of a sitting, I build a refuge tree with the Buddha and all my teachers. I visualize each one, and then feel the particular energetic qualities of each person as I visualize them.

It's a wonderful connection with these beings. When I visualize Dipa Ma, I feel her special combination of emptiness and metta. Her image brings forth a tremendous depth in the heart.

JOSEPH GOLDSTEIN

My practice with Dipa Ma is to place my heart in her care. On one level, I do this by keeping different pictures of her throughout my home and office; on the altar, near my desk, on the screensaver, and on the refrigerator. This way, Dipa Ma is always present, and I can connect with her throughout the day. On another level, I place my heart in her care by recalling the deep nurturance she gave her students. Once on an audiotape of a group at her house in India, I heard her lovingly call to a late-arriving student, who had nowhere to sit, "Come in, please. If there is no room, come sit on my lap. You are my child." Whenever I feel sad, I imagine her calling to me, "Come sit on my lap, my child." In my mind, I go over and put my head on her lap, and she slowly, softly strokes my hair.

AMY SCHMIDT

Through Dipa Ma's death, as with the death of any great teacher, we learn to make her legacy our own. She becomes that light we can orient to so we can do it ourselves.

Where these stories leave off, may your stories begin, and may Ma's benediction guide you on your journey home:

Whatever I have acquired, the strength, the lovingkindness,
I extend to you so that you have faith, so that you are in peace.
By the grace of the Buddha, Dharma, and Sangha,
May everything be good to you,
May you be happy,
May you be protected from harm,
And may you progress in your meditation.
I will always be with you.

AFTERWORD

SINCE DIPA MA'S death, in moments of great difficulty or great inspiration, I've thought of her or evoked her image and felt profoundly touched. Dipa Ma lived the life of the dharma, which meant she paid attention and brought metta to whatever she did. Her presence was that of being respectful for every thing. Her teaching was to "always keep people in your heart." When I am not living fully from body, mind, and heart, her grandmotherly questions arise: "Can you live so that everything you do is blessed? Every joy, every sorrow, every person? Have you let yourself look deeply into what is true?"

In addition to Dipa Ma's inspiration is the power of her being one of our ancestors, in the same way that Ajahn Chah is a Buddhist ancestor for me, and his teacher Ajahn Mun is an ancestor, and the Buddha is an ancestor. Buddhists often evoke the spirit of the Buddha and ask him to teach or guide them, even the ones who intellectually would say, "Well, the Buddha was finished with all his births." In this way you can call upon Dipa Ma as an ancestor through evoking her image or feeling.

Saintly beings, whether they are the Dalai Lama, Mother Teresa, Dipa Ma, or a thousand unknown saintly beings living amongst us, share the same fundamental characteristics of selflessness, great compassion, and peace. Each one of us can carry Dipa Ma's legacy in terms of having that much peace and love. It takes its own time, yet it's possible for anyone. In the end, the point is not to be like Dipa Ma or some other great yogi or saint you might read about. The point is something much more difficult: to be yourself, and to discover that all you seek is to be found, here and now, in your own heart.

Jack Kornfield

ILLUSTRATIONS

CONTRIBUTORS

Dipa Barua is the daughter of Dipa Ma. She is employed by the Central Government in Kolkata (Calcutta) and is involved in many social and religious organizations.

Jyotishmoyee Barua is a housewife in Kolkata and mother of five children.

Pritimoyee Barua is a housewife in Kolkata and mother of two sons.

Rishi Barua is the grandson of Dipa Ma. He received a bachelor's degree from St. Xavier's College, Kolkata, and is studying for his Masters of Commerce degree at Kolkata University.

Sudipti Barua was trained by Dipa Ma as an assistant teacher and helped conduct meditation courses in Bodh Gaya and Kolkata. The mother of six children, she runs a family bakery business in Kolkata.

Roy Bonney is a photographer, body-worker, and counselor in the San Francisco Bay area. He met Dipa Ma in 1973.

Sylvia Boorstein is a founding teacher of Spirit Rock Meditation Center and author of *It's Easier Than You Think: The Buddhist Way to Happiness* and other books on dharma practice.

Daniel Boutemy has been a practicing Theravadan yogi for almost thirty years. He identifies as an openly gay Buddhist and has studied with a variety of teachers in the West and in Asia, in both vipassana and jhana traditions.

Buzz Bussewitz has been a student of insight meditation since

1978 and has made pilgrimages to various sites in Asia, including Tibet. He currently lives in Jamaica Plain, Massachusetts.

Dipak Chowdhury is a bank employee in Kolkata and father of two children. He belongs to various social and religious organizations and is especially committed to projects that aid the poor.

Sukomal Chowdhury, a retired principal and professor of the government Sanskrit College, Kolkata, holds positions in many social and religious organizations. For this book, he translated into English a Bengali publication on Dipa Ma's life.

Howard Cohn has practiced meditation for more than twenty-five years. An original member of the Spirit Rock Teacher Council, he has led meditation retreats worldwide since 1985. His training embraces several traditions, including Theravada, Zen, Dzogchen, and Advaita Vedanta.

Matthew Daniell is a longtime student of insight meditation. He teaches Buddhist meditation and yoga at Tufts University.

Jack Engler is a psychologist who teaches and supervises psychotherapy in the Department of Psychiatry at the Cambridge Hospital and Harvard Medical School. A board member of the Barre Center for Buddhist Studies, he studied with Anagarika Munindra, the Venerable Mahasi Sayadaw, and Thomas Merton. He lives in Massachusetts with his wife and daughter.

Lesley Fowler is a long-term student of insight meditation and the author of books of poetry and fiction. She lives in Australia.

Patricia Genoud-Feldman has been practicing vipassana and Dzogchen in Asia and the West since 1984, and has been teaching internationally since 1997. She is co-founder of the Meditation Center Vimalakirti in Geneva, Switzerland.

Andrew Getz has practiced insight meditation since he was a teenager, including a period of monastic training in Asia. He has a special interest in offering wisdom teachings to at-risk youth through an organization he co-founded called Youth Horizons.

Joseph Goldstein is a co-founder and guiding teacher of Insight Meditation Society. He has been teaching insight meditation retreats worldwide since 1974. The author of several books, including *One Dharma* and *The Experience of Insight,* he is the founder of the Forest Refuge, a center for self-retreat and long-term practice.

David Grant is a middle-school teacher in Portland, Maine, where he lives with his wife and daughter.

Asha Greer is an artist, nurse, senior teacher in the Sufi tradition, and co-founder of the Lama Foundation in New Mexico and the hospice movement in Charlottesville, Virginia. She lives in Batesville, Virginia.

Catherine Ingram is the author of *In the Footsteps of Gandhi* and *Passionate Presence.* She leads Dharma Dialogues and retreats in the United States and Europe.

Myoshin Kelley has been teaching vipassana retreats internationally since 1995. She is the resident teacher at the Forest Refuge, a center for long-term practice at the Insight Meditation Society.

Venerable Khippa-Panno is a Vietnamese monk who has been ordained for over fifty years. He is the abbot at Sakyamuni Meditation Center near Los Angeles and at Jetavan Vihara in Washington, D.C. He has been teaching insight meditation since 1982.

Pamela Kirby is a freelance editor from South Carolina. She lives in Woodacre, California.

Eric Kolvig leads insight meditation retreats and gives talks around the United States. He lives in New Mexico.

Jack Kornfield trained as a Buddhist monk in Asia. He is a founder of Insight Meditation Society and Spirit Rock Meditation Center and has taught meditation internationally since 1974. He has written a number of books on dharma practice, including *A Path with Heart* and *After the Ecstasy, the Laundry.*

Sharon Kreider, a wife and the mother of two children, began insight meditation practice in India in 1977. A licensed therapist working with adolescents and their families, she teaches psychology and stress management at Front Range Community College in Fort Collins, Colorado.

Carol Constantian Lazell began practicing insight meditation at Insight Meditation Society in 1978 and was on the IMS staff from 1981 to 1983. The mother of a teenage daughter, she lives in the San Francisco area and works in an elementary school library.

Michelle and Joel Levey are authors of *Living in Balance, Simple Meditation and Relaxation, Wisdom at Work,* and other books. They have practiced with masters of various Buddhist lineages and teach extensively, taking principles of the dharma into the mainstream through their work with leadership and corporate culture organizations.

Michael Liebenson Grady is a guiding teacher at the Cambridge Insight Meditation Center. He has been practicing insight meditation since 1973.

Jacqueline Mandell is a Buddhist meditation teacher, mother of twin daughters, and president of Leadership from a Pure Heart.

Michele McDonald has practiced insight meditation since 1975 and has taught worldwide since 1982. She has a deep interest in preserving the ancient teachings and in finding ways of expression that make them more accessible in our time.

Maria Monroe began practicing insight meditation with Munindra in Bodh Gaya in 1968 and visited Dipa Ma in Calcutta in 1970. She taught insight meditation from 1979 to 1984. She lives in the Portland, Oregon, area.

Anagarika Munindra was an international meditation teacher. Ordained as a monk under Mahasi Sayadaw, he lived at S. N. Goenka's Vipassana International Academy in Igatpuri, India. He died in 2003.

Sandip Mutsuddi is a father and a state government employee in Kolkata.

Daw Than Myint is Dipa Ma's niece. She is a college teacher in Myanmar.

Susan O'Brien traveled to India with Joseph Goldstein, Sharon Salzberg, and others in 1979 when they visited Dipa Ma in Bodh Gaya and at her home in Calcutta. Susan began teaching meditation in 1996 and coordinates the Insight Meditation correspondence course.

Wendy Palmer has practiced Aikido and meditation for over thirty years. She is the author of *The Intuitive Body* and *The Practice of Freedom*.

Venerable Rastrapala Mahathera is president of the Vipassana International Meditation Center in Bodh Gaya, where he named the meditation hall in memory of Dipa Ma. He is a writer and a teacher of insight meditation.

Bob Ray is the co-founder with his wife Dixie of the Southwest Center for Spiritual Living. Bob leads a weekly sitting group in Las Vegas, New Mexico.

Sharda Rogell has practiced in the Theravadan tradition since 1979 and has taught worldwide since 1985. Influenced by Advaita Vedanta and Dzogchen, she brings a strong emphasis to awakening heartfulness.

Janice Rubin is a Houston-based photographer whose work has been published and exhibited internationally since 1976. Her exhibit and book *The Mikvah Project* (which explores the ancient and secret Jewish women's ritual bath) continues its tour across North America.

Sharon Salzberg is a co-founder of the Insight Meditation Society, where she is one of the guiding teachers. She has practiced Buddhist meditation since 1970 and has taught worldwide since 1974. She is the author of several books, including *Faith: Trusting Your Own Deepest Experience* and *Lovingkindness: The Revolutionary Art of Happiness.*

Katrina Schneider studied extensively in a forest monastery in Burma under the guidance of Taungpulu Sayadaw. She currently lives in the United States and uses meditation in her work with hospice patients and people suffering from chronic pain.

Steven Schwartz has been practicing insight meditation for over thirty years and is one of the founders of Insight Meditation Society. He was a student of Dipa Ma for most of this period and hosted her first trip to the United States.

Steven Smith is co-founder of Vipassana Hawaii and a guiding teacher at Insight Meditation Society. He leads retreats worldwide.

Janne Stark is a hearth-tender and mother, an infant-toddler childcare provider, and a farmers' market manager. She leads a meditation group in Portland, Oregon.

Ajahn Thanasanti was introduced to Buddhist meditation in 1979 in a class taught by Jack Engler. Ten years later, she went to Amaravati Buddhist Monastery in England where she took novice precepts. In 1991, she was ordained as a Buddhist nun with Ajahn Sumedho as her preceptor.

Kate ("Lila") Wheeler attended her first Buddhist retreat in 1977. She has written a novel, *When Mountains Walked,* and a book of short stories, *Not Where I Started From,* as well as articles for the *New York Times, Tricycle: The Buddhist Review,* and other publications. She lives in Massachusetts.

Carol Wilson has been practicing meditation since 1971. She studied with a variety of teachers, including practice as a Buddhist nun in Thailand. She has been teaching internationally since 1986.

Author

Amy Schmidt was a resident teacher at the Insight Meditation Society in Barre, Massachusetts, and a co-founder of Southwest Sangha, a self-retreat center in southern New Mexico. Amy is also a licensed clinical social worker. Her cartoons appear in *Buddha Laughing* (Bell Tower, 1999).

Editors

Don Morreale is the editor of *The Complete Guide to Buddhist America.* A long-term dharma student and freelance writer, he lives in Denver, Colorado.

Madelaine Fahrenwald is a freelance editor and long-term dharma student.

Special thanks to these individuals who worked on *Knee Deep in Grace:* Ann Lowe, Joy Fox, Denise Gibson, and especially Sara Jenkins as publisher.